ALT

Usable Knowledge

USABLE KNOWLEDGE

Social Science and Social
Problem Solving

Charles E. Lindblom and
David K. Cohen

New Haven and London   Yale University Press

Library of Congress catalog card number: 78–65494
International standard book number: 0–300–02335–9 (clothbound); 0–300–
02336–7 (paperbound)
Set in Times Roman type.
Printed in the United States of America by
The Vail-Ballou Press, Binghamton, N.Y.

Published in Great Britain, Europe, Africa, and
Asia (except Japan) by Yale University Press,
Ltd., London. Distributed in Australia and
New Zealand by Book & Film Services, Artarmon,
N.S.W., Australia; and in Japan by Harper & Row,
Publishers, Tokyo Office.

Contents

Preface

The stimulus that gives rise to this book is dissatisfaction with social science and social research as instruments of social problem solving. Policy makers and other practical problem solvers frequently voice their frustration with what they are offered. And many social scientists and social researchers seem to wish to be more drawn upon, useful, or influential.

To make headway against this problem, we believe that social scientists and social researchers must first understand their own professional practices, which are obscured by habitual confusion between what they actually do and what conventional scientific conventions persuade them that they must be—because they ought to be—doing. In this book, we take a step. We suggest the kinds of questions that social scientists and researchers need to ask about their own work if they wish to understand it better as a possible contribution not only to policy making but to other forms of social problem solving. It is only a small step, but in taking it we join a growing number of colleagues who are opening up significant issues bearing on the usefulness, both in the short run and in the very long run, of social science and research for social problem solving. We also offer a lengthy bibliography intended to facilitate work on these issues.

Both of us came to this interest through an outgrowth of our own earlier work. That we could achieve a fruitful collaboration seems even more improbable after the event than before. One of us is by training and style of thought given to history and to the interconnection of phenomena that will not remain separate to suit the analyst's convenience. The other is ahistorical, prefers the cross-sectional slice to unfolding sequences, and pushes toward sharpness of distinction easier to record on paper than to find in the real world. Although our collaboration has been illuminating as well as cordial, happy, and sometimes exhilarating, it has not been easy.

We wish to record our thanks to a number of helpful colleagues, with most of whom we have been joined in highly profitable discussion in Yale's Institution for Social and Policy Studies: Paul Burstein, David R. Cameron, Joan Costello, Robert A. Dahl, Leonard W. Doob, Stephen P. Dresch, James W. Fesler, James S. Fishkin, Wendell R. Garner, Patricia A. Graham, Judith E. Gruber, J. Richard Hackman, Eric A. Hanushek, Everett C. Ladd, David R. Mayhew, Richard R. Nelson, Guy H. Orcutt, Edward W. Pauly, Douglas W. Rae, Albert J. Reiss, Jr., James E. Rosenbaum, Seymour B. Sarason, John G. Simon, Edison J. Trickett, Carol H. Weiss, Edward J. Woodhouse, and Douglas T. Yates. We are especially grateful to Janet A. Weiss, both for helpful discussion and detailed comments on an earlier draft. In addition, we record our appreciation of help from a number of graduate students: Randall J. Billington, James Galbraith, Michael Sabia, James Swiss, Jeffrey T. Wack, Adair L. Waldenberg, and Ted I. K. Youn. For editorial assistance we are indebted to Richard Smithey. We take particular pleasure in recording our gratitude to P. Robin Ellis for a range of secretarial services, including typing the manuscript, performed with skill, thoughtfulness, intelligence, and productive good will.

1. The Study of Social Science as an Instrument of Social Problem Solving

In public policy making, many suppliers and users of social research are dissatisfied, the former because they are not listened to, the latter because they do not hear much they want to listen to.[1] Out of the discontent a river of mixed diagnosis and prescription now flows: case studies, reflections on experience, conference reports, and some "hard" research—all adding up to hundreds of papers, a scattering of books, and a handful of commission reports.[2]

Excellent as some of these contributions are, an attribute of some of them is their blind man's view of the elephant. Some, for example, take note only of social research that is directly addressed to a policy maker's problem, as though assuming that no other kind of social science or social research enters into social problem solving.[3] Others

1. See, for testimony, the papers in Carol H. Weiss, *Using Social Research for Public Policy Making* (Lexington, Mass.: D. C. Heath & Co., 1977), esp. p. 5. Increasingly, however, it is being noted that governmental users of social research use it in ways other than those intended by the researchers.

2. For some thoughtful and comprehensive surveys of social science and research in relation to social problem solving, see, among others: National Academy of Sciences, *The Behavioral Sciences and the Federal Government* (Washington, D.C., 1968); U.S. National Science Foundation, *Knowledge into Action: Improving the Nation's Use of the Social Sciences* (Washington, D.C., Report of the Special Commission on the Social Sciences, 1968); and the National Academy of Sciences and the Social Science Research Council, *The Behavioral and Social Sciences: Outlook and Needs* (Washington, D.C., 1969). See also publications of the current National Academy of Sciences and National Research Council study project on social research and development.

Many of the most useful essays, studies, and other contributions are listed in the Bibliography.

3. For an example, see Harold Wilensky, *Organizational Intelligence*

see the problem as one of inadequate utilization of available social research, assuming that we already possess satisfactory knowledge that policy makers will not, for various perverse reasons, use.[4] Others assert that the problem lies in unsatisfactory personal relations between social researchers and client, forgetting that in most uses of social research no personal researcher-client relationship exists at all, the user simply drawing on published work of faceless social scientists.[5] Others are parochial because arbitrarily timebound. They assume that the problem is one of an inadequate relationship between contemporary social researchers and their counterpart problem solvers in government, without thought of the possibility that the most fruitful collaboration may be between the social scientists of an earlier generation and policy makers of a later one. And, as a final example, some conceive of the problem cosmetically: social scientists do not write attractively.

The error of these and other parochial views is in confusing the part with the whole. Seen as a whole, obstacles to and potentials for more useful social science and research pose profound questions about man as a problem

---

(New York: Basic Books, 1976). For another example, see Nathan Caplan, *The Use of Social Science Knowledge in Policy Decisions at the National Level* (University of Michigan Center for Research on Utilization of Scientific Knowledge, 1975). In that study, interviews with 204 officials elicited testimony of 575 instances of their use of social science knowledge. In all 575 instances, only contemporary specialized studies were mentioned, as though no other social science resources existed to draw upon. One has to assume that the questionnaire so directed the respondents. Yet the report makes no mention of such a restriction, from which we infer that the research team responsible for the study simply ignored without self-awareness all but the tip of the iceberg.

4. As noted by Robert F. Rich, "Uses of Social Science Information by Federal Bureaucrats: Knowledge for Action versus Knowledge for Understanding," in Weiss, *Using Social Research in Public Policy Making*, pp. 199—211, and esp. p. 207.

5. For an example, see Paul F. Lazarsfeld, William H. Sewell, and Harold L. Wilensky, eds., *The Uses of Sociology* (New York: Basic Books, 1967), p. x.

solver, about knowledge and craft, about science, and about a complex social and political order in which knowledge and science are embedded and by which they are shaped. In the larger view, tedious questions about research and policy making are transformed into challenging questions about man, his brain, politics, and society. It is on these questions that inquiry is required, no less so than on immediate questions of research design. Our purpose in these pages is to outline such an inquiry—that is, to propose issues for investigation.

Our book has a touch of oddity about it. It does not offer sustained discussion on any issue raised. Instead, it goes no further with each issue raised than to indicate that it poses a challenge to research. Everything in it should be read as a proposal, question, or hypothesis. It sums up, not to an extended or tested analysis, but to a research program that we both set for ourselves and commend to our colleagues who study social problem solving, policy making, policy analysis, and the place of social science and social research in them. As we move on through the pages of the book, we do not weary the reader with constant repetition of "This issue needs to be researched" or "This hypothesis needs testing" or "Further questions need to be raised about this aspect of social science." But that is the point of these pages—to identify issues and to give them a coherent organization and motivation.

In the literature, the kind of questions we raise are usually put as questions about government policy making. We shall instead inquire more abstractly and inclusively into social problem solving. Doing so will permit us to consider social science and social research not only in their governmental uses but in their uses by people in business enterprises and other private groups or by anyone who takes some responsibility for ameliorating or solving a social problem. We shall use the term "problem solver" to refer to any such person, exclusive of persons engaged in professional social science and research.

By social problem solving, we mean processes that are thought to eventuate in outcomes that by some standard are an improvement on the previously existing situation, or are presumed to so eventuate, or are conceived of as offering some possibility to so eventuate. We do not limit the term to processes that achieve ideal or even satisfactory outcomes; and in that light, "problem-attacking" is more accurate a term than "problem-solving." Nor do we limit the term to the intellectual processes through which people grapple with problems. Coin tossing is also a problem-solving activity. Some students of problem solving hold that "solve" implies understanding, as in solving a mathematical problem. For us, "solve" does not require an understanding of "the problem" but only an outcome, as when coin tossing solves a problem of whether to turn left or right at an unfamiliar, unmarked road junction.

A few contributors to the discussion of the unsatisfactory record of social research in social problem solving have tackled some of the most profound questions—Marx, Weber, Dewey, and Mannheim among them.[6] But their theoretical contributions have not been drawn into the swelling "practical" discussion of the specific difficulties encountered by social scientists when they take part in social problem solving. Hence, an identification of major issues about research and social problem solving, which is what we here attempt, is designed both to suggest directions for the contemporary "practical" investigation and to enrich that investigation with the older tradition of theory.

We do not assume that social science and social research should always—or even most often—be designed for or

6. For example, Max Weber, "Politics As A Vocation" (1918) reprinted in H. H. Gerth and C. Wright Mills, *From Max Weber* (New York: Oxford University Press, 1946); John Dewey, *The Quest for Certainty* (New York: Pulman, 1929); and Karl Mannheim, *Ideology and Utopia* (1929) (New York: Harcourt, Brace and World, 1936).

tested by their usefulness for social problem solving. We assume only that much is so designed or unintentionally achieves such an effect. For that share, questions about its contribution to social problem solving are important questions.

How do we define "useful" or "success" or "failure?" What are our criteria for judging the impact of social science and research to be large or small, successful or not, useful or not? The exploration of answers to these questions is a very large part of the research to be done. We can illustrate why.

Several studies of social science impact report that policy makers cannot point to instances in which their decisions were directly altered by a specific relevant study.[7] A failure? Not necessarily. As some studies are beginning to perceive, other indirect and lagged influences can be found. We suggest a rough parallel to illustrate one such impact. Kuhn and others have explored the effects of specific scientific studies that test major scientific frameworks or theories. Any one specific study, even though it appears to invalidate a standing theory or framework of understanding, *fails* to do so. Faced by conflict between the results of the test study and the prevailing theory, scientists reject the study rather than the theory. Only a succession and a variety of invalidating studies can erode the validity of established belief, at which point it is supplanted by a new theory, framework, or, in Kuhn's word, paradigm.[8] By parallel, it may be that the principal impact of policy-oriented studies, say, on inflation, race conflict, deviance, or foreign policy— including those specifically designed to advise a specific policy maker at a particular time—is through their con-

7. Michael Q. Patton et al., "In Search of Impact," in Weiss, *Using Social Research*.

8. Thomas S. Kuhn, *The Structure of Scientific Revolutions*, 2d ed. (Chicago: University of Chicago Press, 1970), esp. chaps. 6, 7, and 8.

tribution to a cumulating set of incentives for a general reconsideration by policy makers of their decision-making framework, their operating political or social philosophy, or their ideology.

We are in no position to define or judge usefulness or failure until various kinds of possible usefulness are explored in continuing research.

In raising questions for research on research itself, we think it appropriate to go to the very fundamentals of social science as an instrument of social problem solving. We suggest that social science and social research are only weakly understood by their own practitioners (ourselves included) and that the practice of them is crippled by that misunderstanding. We do not exclude the possibility that social scientists (ourselves included) hold a fundamentally wrong conception of social science. One reason for this state of affairs is that practitioners have not applied the tools of their trade to the trade itself. This programmatic essay is an attempt to help open up the possibility for such an application.[9]

9. Much of the argument in these pages is closely related to Lindblom's earlier work on policy making: specifically, on disjointed incrementalism and partisan mutual adjustment. The earlier work, however, took the practices of most social scientists largely for granted and turned its attention exclusively to those social scientists and other analysts who directly grapple with policy issues. Our present purpose is much broader. It is to raise questions about the general practice of social research, thus about the practices of social scientists generally, and about the relation of social science to other kinds of professional and nonprofessional inquiry into the social world, as well as into explicit policy questions. Our concern with social science and social research as contributors to social problem solving encompasses not merely policy analysis, as did the earlier work, but all social problem solving. Marx, Durkheim, Weber, and Parsons are grist for our mill no less than staff researchers or contracted social scientists working for the U.S. Department of Health, Education, and Welfare.

Where the earlier studies largely focused on issues about the policy-making process, the studies proposed here largely focus on methodological problems in social science and social research. More precisely, where the earlier studies examined an intersection of social science and policy making, an intersection engaging only a periphery of each, the proposed

THE DOMAIN OF SOCIAL SCIENCE AND SOCIAL RESEARCH

Many professional investigators of the social world engage in what is commonly called social science. Yet many of their investigations are not of a kind that most academic social scientists would regard as social science. We would prefer not to beg any questions by claiming, through terminological convention, that all of the various kinds of studies, analyses, and research activities that we want to examine are scientific. We want to be free to raise questions not only about academic social science but about the larger variety of investigatory activities. The phenomenon to be investigated, then, is *professional social inquiry* (of many kinds) and its role in social problem solving.

Consider the variety: evaluation studies carried out in profit-making firms; opinion research in commercial survey organizations; university-trained policy analysts working in government offices; newspaper and TV reporters specialized in some aspect of social science germane to their beats; development and dissemination work aimed at solving social problems carried out in specialized R&D "laboratories" in education or mental health.

Few of these activities bear the most important hallmarks of social science—among them a concern with extending theory, a focus on causal explanation of social phenomena, and intimate connection between the work at hand and preexisting research and theory. Yet they do have some important features in common with academic social science. First, all are indebted for some of their methodology to social science. Second, they are carried out by professionals. Third, almost all aspire to "authoritative-

---

studies move back from the periphery in the direction of the center of social science.

It turns out, however, that some of the same issues earlier raised about analysis of explicit policy issues now need to be raised about social science more generally. Some of these issues, as they earlier appeared, will therefore be familiar from the earlier context.

ness" by virtue of an association with science. Professional social inquiry (PSI) thus includes:[10]

1. The work of seminal minds like Marx, Freud, and Adam Smith
2. Academic social science, tentatively defined as what academic social scientists do in their specialized roles
3. The following overlapping activities, whether pursued by academic social scientists or others:

   Sustained, systematic, and professional classification, conceptualization, development and testing of nomothetic and other substantial generalizations, development and testing of theories (defined as logically interlocked sets of generalizations)

   Highly systematic data gathering and reporting (census, much though not all survey research, and ethnological fieldwork are examples)[11]

   Statistical manipulation and analysis of social data

   Mathematical and other modeling of social processes

   Many but not all historical works

   Social commentary and criticism

   Systematic professional speculative thought

   Policy analyses in which problem is defined, goals and other values are specified, alternative solutions are canvassed and analyzed, and policy recommendations are reached

   Policy analyses in which only part of such a task is systematically and professionally attempted

   Systematic search for specific information or data thought to be important (either by supplier or potential user) for a forthcoming decision

   Systematic professional analysis of any aspect of society,

---

10. We hope that readers will excuse both the use of "PSI," for professional social inquiry, as well as "pPSI," referring to people who do it. Awkward, yes; but less so, we trust, than constant reiteration of the much longer terms they abbreviate.

11. In the list, the frequent use of the terms "systematic" and "professional" is intended to separate occasional and superficially practiced activities such as classification, conceptualization, generalization, speculation, fact-gathering, and policy analysis, in which all people engage, from the presumably more sustained, elaborate, and skilled practice of these activities by professional persons bearing such designation as social scientist, statistician, systems analyst, or researcher. But we remain open to the argument that the difference is often extremely small or even nonexistent.

whether designed to illuminate some aspect of the social world
or to make a contribution to the solution of a social problem

Operations research and systems analysis on social problems, and
other specialized activities like input-output analysis,
mathematical programming, and cost-effectiveness analysis

Policy evaluation

Consulting services by professionals

Any or all of the above, pursued either within a single discipline
or across disciplinary lines, and by individuals, teams or organizations

Any of the above, pursued independently of, or together with,
scientific or engineering studies (for example, studies of
medical-care policy, of problems in human performance in
spacecraft, or environmental problems)

Any intellectual activities necessary to any of the above and
consequently made part of any of the above

It is clear from the list that we are interested in the
contribution made to social problem solving by both pure
or basic PSI, on one hand, and applied PSI, on the
other—whatever the two terms mean.[12] This is not to be
simply a study of applied social research.

12. They are discussed in chapter 6 below.

2. The Relation of Professional Social Inquiry to Other Inputs into Social Problem Solving

Information and analysis constitute only one route among several to social problem solving. And PSI is one method among several of providing information and analysis to the extent that they are required. Information and analysis provide only one route because, we shall suggest, a great deal of the world's problem solving is and ought to be accomplished through various forms of social interaction that substitute action for thought, understanding, or analysis. Information and analysis are not a universal or categorical prescription for social problem solving. In addition, PSI is only one among several analytical methods, because other forms of information and analysis—ordinary knowledge and casual analysis foremost among them—are often sufficient or better than PSI for social problem solving. In this chapter we shall briefly lay out our reasons for so characterizing PSI as only one among several routes to social problem solving.

We suggest that many practitioners misconceive of PSI because explicitly or implicitly they deny the above propositions. Some practitioners of PSI (pPSI) appear to believe that, ideally, social problem solving is a scientific activity, hence in the real world PSI is the best method of approaching social problems, and is so far superior to all others as to warrant disregard of them, except as they inescapably appear sometimes as poor substitutes. To be sure, most pPSI allow some room for a nonscientific component in social problem solving, one that is necessary for choosing, defining, or postulating goals and other values that cannot be established by science without confusing "is" with "ought." But beyond that, social problem solving comes to be largely identified in their minds with a rationalistic, scientific, intellectual investigatory process.

Perhaps more than other social scientists, political scientists understand that conflict over values demands what they would call "political" rather than analytical problem solving.[1] But that has not dissuaded some political scientists from making sometimes extravagant endorsements of analytical problem solving as preferable wherever possible. And for problem solving not marked by values conflict, they have often simply assumed the categorical superiority of analytical over political problem solving, at an extreme—which most political scientists do not reach—treating political problem solving as the recourse of societies that have not yet learned the virtues of policy making through analysis rather than through partisan politics.

Of those pPSI who acknowledge that various kinds of social interaction are necessary to social problem solving —that analysis cannot do it all—and who consequently claim an appropriately reduced role for information and analysis, many fall into the error of assuming that, insofar as information and analysis *are* called for, the call is ideally for PSI, to the exclusion of ordinary knowledge, casual empiricism, and other nonscientific or nonprofessional methods of knowing and analyzing.

Misperceptions in these various versions are sometimes explicitly stated, as we shall see. But more often they appear as working assumptions.

The issue—whether practitioners of PSI go wrong in believing that it is central to social problem solving when it is actually only one of several no less important inputs—is thus posed. To show that this is an important issue worthy of sustained study requires some preliminary argument and

1. An excellent statement is in James G. March and Herbert A. Simon, *Organizations* (New York: John Wiley, 1958), pp. 129ff.

evidence that in good social problem solving:

a. PSI is in fact only one among several equally important routes to solutions.
b. Many pPSI believe that it is the only or the main route.
c. Their misperception leads them astray and calls for reconsideration of the practice of PSI.

We shall attend to each of these three allegations. As for the third, we shall suggest that the effect of the misperception is to lead practitioners to attempt too many tasks indiscriminately, to expend energies on tasks they cannot do as well as on those they need not do at all, and thus to fail to focus on those tasks for which PSI is especially suited and needed.

PSI AND ORDINARY KNOWLEDGE

To begin with, pPSI greatly overestimate the amount and distinctiveness of the information and analysis they offer for social problem solving. They greatly underestimate the society's use—and necessary use—of an existing stock, as well as a flow of new ordinary knowledge from sources other than pPSI.

By "ordinary knowledge," we mean knowledge that does not owe its origin, testing, degree of verification, truth status, or currency to distinctive PSI professional techniques but rather to common sense, casual empiricism, or thoughtful speculation and analysis. It is highly fallible, but we shall call it knowledge even if it is false. As in the case of scientific knowledge, whether it is true or false, knowledge is knowledge to anyone who takes it as a basis for some commitment or action.

For social problem solving, we suggest, people will always depend heavily on ordinary knowledge. Ordinary knowledge tells us that legislatures make laws and perform certain other functions, some public officials take bribes, most families in industrial societies are nuclear rather than extended, wheat farmers will restrict production if paid to do so, children become angry when thwarted, and so on. Indeed, our dependence on ordinary information goes further than that. It is ordinary knowledge that tells us so fundamental a fact as that the moving forms we see about us displaying shape and movement like ours are human beings much like ourselves. It is ordinary knowledge that tells us that when we hear the word *crime*, the speaker is probably referring to law-breaking behavior of certain categories. The most basic knowledge we use in social problem solving is ordinary.[2]

Everyone has ordinary knowledge—has it, uses it, offers it. It is not, however, a homogeneous commodity. Some ordinary knowledge, most people would say, is more reliable, more probably true, than other. People differ from each other in the kind and quality of ordinary knowledge they possess. Yet although pPSI possess a great amount of relatively high-quality ordinary knowledge, so do many journalists, civil servants, businessmen, interest-group leaders, public opinion leaders, and elected officials. Practitioners of PSI may have no distinctive advantages in stock or use of ordinary knowledge helpful to public policy and many other forms of social problem solving. If they do, just what the advantages are needs to be identified.

But practitioners of PSI attest that they offer more than

---

2. Several of our colleagues, Judith Gruber, Giandomenico Majone, Edward Pauly, and Janet Weiss, call our attention to skill and craft as forms of knowledge different from ordinary knowledge. And if knowledge is characterized by how it is developed or processed, then certain kinds of knowledge produced in legal proceedings is, again, different from ordinary knowledge. Moreover, ordinary knowledge itself may be of sharply differing kinds. Some of it was once scientific knowledge. Some of it takes the form of norms rather than facts. If, for example, we establish routines or norms for coping with certain problems—establishing a fire drill, for example—we would say we as a result now *know* how to cope with a fire. If that, however, is ordinary knowledge, it is perhaps different from garden-variety ordinary knowledge. In short, the use of the concept of ordinary knowledge calls for exploration in many directions.

ordinary knowledge. They claim that they have pushed on to knowledge available exclusively to them because they practice professional investigatory techniques not used by the casual empiricist. Moreover, they claim to have tested some of the content of ordinary knowledge and rejected some of it that is in error, setting in its place, consequently, more reliable information than is known to persons other than themselves.

We grant the claim—on both counts. But, we suggest, it amounts to a much smaller claim than is often supposed. It is a much smaller claim, for instance, than that of the social science enthusiast who sees himself as contributing to an eventual from-the-ground-up replacement of ordinary by scientific knowledge. Moreover, it says only that at least *some* of the work of pPSI has the effect of reshaping somewhat the mountain of ordinary knowledge. Such a claim, we suggest, sharply reduces the supposed distinctive advantage of PSI over other sources of information and analysis for social problem solving.

PSI as Supplement to Ordinary Knowledge

To clarify what distinctive contribution PSI makes, then, calls for a further specification of just how it relates as a supplement to ordinary knowledge.

1. For a pPSI, we suggest that most of the knowledge which appears in his work is ordinary knowledge that is widely dispersed among relatively informed members of society and not the product of PSI inquiry or verification. That businessmen will not invest if earnings are not anticipated, that in many circumstances prices and wages spiral upward together, that disciplinary problems in schools distract teachers from educational work, that medical practice in the U.S.A. is at a high technical level (and that some doctors take kickbacks), and that television absorbs much of the time of children are widely known (or believed) propositions. Of many important propositions like these,

pPSI know no more than many other informed members of our society. Nor can they usually offer more verified versions of such propositions than others can, although they can provide some degree of verification for a few of the many propositions they present.

2. Moreover, much of the "new" knowledge produced by pPSI is ordinary knowledge. That is to say, it is produced by the same common techniques of speculation and casual verification that are practiced throughout the society by many different kinds of people, and is not by any significant margin more firmly verified. Despite the professional development of specialized investigative techniques, especially quantitative, most practitioners of professional social inquiry, including the most distinguished among them, inevitably rely heavily on the same ordinary techniques of speculation, definition, conceptualization, hypothesis formulation, and verification as are practiced by persons who are not social scientists or professional investigators of any kind.

These pPSI often practice the techniques with professional skill but the techniques themselves are the same as those of casual empiricism and ordinary analysis. Quantitative and mathematical social scientists like James Coleman, Kenneth Arrow, and Tjalling Koopmans display these ordinary methods among their more specialized ones. Many other social scientists work almost entirely with the ordinary methods: for example, Joseph Schumpeter, Talcott Parsons, Robert Merton, and Albert Hirschman. In reading their work, one only rarely comes across statistical or other differentiated techniques special to PSI or to scientific investigation. Many of their propositions are verified no more and no less than many of the propositions of ordinary knowledge from other sources.

Scientific observation is deliberate search, carried out with care and forethought, as contrasted with the casual and largely passive perceptions of everyday life. It is this deliberateness and control of the process of observation that is distinctive of science, not merely the use of special instruments (important as they are)—save as this use is itself indicative of forethought and care. Tycho Brahe was one of the greatest of astronomical observers though he had no telescope; Darwin also relied heavily on the naked eye; De Toqueville was a superb observer without any of the data-gathering devices of contemporary social research.[3]

3. When practitioners of PSI push on to new knowledge significant for social problem solving, they can produce, we suggest, no more than a small number of propositions —tiny compared with the stock of propositions commonly employed in social problem solving. That is to say, their offered increment of new knowledge is just a veneer or, again, an addition to a mountainous body of knowledge.

4. We further suggest that part of the new PSI knowledge generated by investigatory techniques distinctive to PSI is an even smaller flow, perhaps better characterized as a trickle.

5. The distinctive techniques of PSI, we suggest, are more often used to test existing propositions growing out of and circulating as ordinary knowledge. Hence, with these techniques PSI refines ordinary knowledge more than it creates new previously unformulated knowledge.

6. When it refines it does so selectively—indeed highly selectively. The number of propositions drawn from ordinary knowledge that are subjected to distinctive PSI forms of testing represents an extremely small fraction of the knowledge used by pPSI in their work and of knowledge for social problem solving. And as for propositions thus tested, which as a consequence can be said to have been

---

3. Abraham Kaplan, *The Conduct of Inquiry* (San Francisco: Chandler Publishing Co., 1964), p. 126.

given a high degree of verification, their number is extraordinarily restricted. One is hard-pressed to think of examples.

Consequently, PSI is not broadly a distinctive source of information and analysis; it is only occasionally so. In saying this, we do not intend to slight the effects that PSI sometimes appears to exert on social problem solving. We quickly acknowledge that the veneer of and the occasional verification of knowledge may often be critical, crucial, or pivotal. We do, however, want to suggest the relation of PSI to a mountain of ordinary information which it cannot replace but only reshape here and there.

It may be worth noting further that on those selected occasions when pPSI seek either to extend or test knowledge by scientific practice, they must lean heavily on ordinary knowledge in the very process of verification. Science can proceed only by trusting and using a vast amount of ordinary knowledge, often using it to discredit some part of it. Taking as an example a scientific paper on the quantum nature of light, Campbell writes:

> a common-sense, prescientific perception of objects, solids, and light was employed and trusted in coming to the conclusions that revise the ordinary understanding. To challenge and correct the common-sense understanding in one detail, common-sense understanding in general has to be trusted.[4]

A scientist engaged in so objective a measurement process as applying a ruler to a line to determine its length must call on ordinary knowledge to tell him that the length of the line does not change during the measurement and that his particular ruler is not elastic.[5]

---

4. Donald T. Campbell, "Qualitative Knowing in Action Research," *Journal of Social Issues*, forthcoming.
5. Ibid.

Preliminary Inferences

Inferences of this long line of argument for the practice of PSI seem so highly persuasive that they might as well be immediately acknowledged in advance of later chapters: among others, that PSI should be more discriminatingly focused; the pPSI should develop, as we shall later see in more detail, critical or pivotal interventions in social problem solving rather than the comprehensive studies often advocated for policy analysis; and that pPSI should study and develop possible cooperative relationships with other sources of the ordinary information on which they themselves heavily depend.

SOCIAL LEARNING AS AN ALTERNATIVE TO PSI AND OTHER KINDS OF ANALYSIS

Another input into social problem solving which offers an alternative to PSI is often what we shall call, for want of a better name, social learning. It is not much discussed as a method of problem solving. We have found no more than passing reference to it as a possible alternative to PSI. Practitioners deny its importance not by explicit allegation but by ignoring the possibility, when they set directions for their own work, that it renders their research unnecessary.

In contemporary America and Western Europe, inflation appears to be an example of a problem that cannot be solved until certain groups of people learn different behavior. Some of the contesting groups in the population (businessmen and wage earners, for example), it may turn out, must decrease their demands for income. Energy conservation may be another example: an effective conservation policy may be impossible until various groups learn new behavior.

Until the required learning occurs, PSI may be futile. For the learning we have in mind in such cases comes from actual experience that upsets old attitudes and dispositions. We have already noted that PSI itself can sometimes upset them (p.17), but sometimes not. In that case, social learning does not come from the communication of new information and analysis accomplished through PSI. In the case of energy policy, it would come from paying high prices for fuel, or waiting in long lines at gasoline stations, or from the discomfort of cold housing, not from facts or predictions on fuel shortage or analysis of hypothetical alternatives.

PSI is ineffective or irrelevant in such a situation except to the degree it can be made a supplement to the required social learning as, for example, by answering questions that arise after and as a result of the learning. It cannot be a substitute for the required learning, neither can it contribute greatly to it. The requirement for a solution to the problem is the actual experience that leads to reconsidered positions rather than a professional investigator's examination of the existing circumstance or of feasible policies (that do not yet exist). The common opinion "things will have to get worse before they get better" testifies to the possibility that a problem cannot be solved until people have had—or suffered—such experiences as will bring them to new attitudes and political dispositions.

When experimental social learning is required and when as an alternative PSI is or is not possible, is not something easily known. We suggest that the alternatives exist, however, and warrant study.

INTERACTION AS AN ALTERNATIVE TO PSI

Another alternative to PSI is interactive problem solving through the many devices by which action substitutes for thought—never wholly but significantly. In exploring interactive problem solving, we shall come to understand better the relation of thought to action. We can thus give some specific content to familiar and somewhat empty declarations that analysts of social problems must see their problems in their political and social context.

Analytical and Interactive Problem Solving

Here for terminological convenience we need to draw a distinction between what we shall call analytical problem solving and interactive problem solving. We set out as one alternative the attempt by "society" or its policy makers to solve a given problem or improve a situation through someone's understanding the situation and its possible remedies so that a solution or preferred outcome can be decided upon. The other alternative is—as in tossing a coin to decide a question—to undertake or stimulate action— usually interaction—so that the preferred outcome comes about without anyone's having analyzed the given problem or having achieved an analyzed solution to it. A given problem can be attacked by understanding, thought, or analysis (we treat these terms as strictly synonymous) of that very problem, or by various forms of interaction among people, in which what they do, rather than what they or anyone else thinks (or understands or analyzes) about that problem moves toward the solution or preferred situation. Strictly speaking, since people never stop thinking, the alternatives are a frontal analytical attack on some identified problem, or interaction in which thought or analysis is adapted to the interaction and is therefore on some issues displaced by interaction.

Everyone knows that we are all constantly engaged in social interaction. But we do not well understand that interaction is a method of problem solving: we see the phenomenon—we can hardly miss it—but not its function in problem solving. In fact, we are quick to see that interaction obviously often brings about, causes, or itself constitutes a problem. Examples are mugging, careless driving, or arrogant bureaucratic behavior. And we often see interaction as required not in solving a problem but in implementation of a solution, as when aldermen analytically reach a decision as to which streets they will resurface and then set up a complex pattern of administrative interactions to carry out their decisions: contracts, hiring workers, rerouting traffic during repairs, and paying the bills, for example. But our interest is in interaction as an alternative to understanding, thought, or analysis, thus as a way of finding an outcome that can be considered a solution to a problem. That is what tossing a coin is—a simple form of action rather than thought. It reaches an outcome. It solves the problem of whether to go right or left at an unmarked, unfamiliar road junction. And it may do so faster, no more fallibly, and no less efficiently than can an analyzed solution.

Often one and the same interaction can be seen in different ways. For most of us, mugging is a problem. For some extreme critics of the established social order, it is a solution—a way in which the problem of unequal income is ameliorated. For the mugger, it is a way of implementing a solution to his problem of inadequate income, a solution reached through his own analysis of the options open to him. We are interested in those interactions that are worth considering as a method of solving a problem— interactions that are an alternative to bringing understanding, thought, or analysis frontally to bear on that problem.

Although coin tossing is a frequently useful alternative to analysis, the kinds of interactions that concern us are more complex. An example is voting. Elections substitute action for thought on some issues even if each voter decides his own vote thoughtfully. That is so because the particular problem of how to reconcile or aggregate many diverse preferences into a collective decision, which is an aspect of the larger problem of choosing a president, is solved not by any thought or analysis directed to that particular problem but by complex actions—voting, counting ballots, authorizing the candidates who, by some rule, win. In the U.S.A., the question of who should be made president is a ''what to do'' problem that might be solved by PSI. Instead it is solved in large part by an elaborate ceremony of action.

We may note that the ceremony is established by rules, and the rules are the product of prior analysis (but also, to some degree, of custom). But for the recurring problem of how to convert disparate preferences or volitions into a decision on who should be president, on that particular problem interaction provides the solution. In other words, a solution to that particular problem is reached, but not as a result of anyone's analyzing *that* problem through to a solution.[6]

In market societies, the problem of determining the goods and services to which the nation's resources should be allocated provides another familiar major example of interactive problem solving. That problem is "solved" as a by-product of countless acts of buying and selling. One can set in contrast a hypothetical system (or real-world system like the USSR) in which the resource allocation problem is assigned to planners who are expected to approach it by explicit and frontal analysis directed toward it. They solve the problem with analysis of the problem. In solving the same problem by market interactions, analysis need only attend to limited questions—for example, a businessman's question about what to produce or sell or a policy maker's question about whether market structure is such as to produce efficient market interactions.

It perhaps illuminates the endless variety of interactive methods of social problem solving to observe that, when market interactions do not give us acceptable solutions, we often turn not to direct frontal analysis but to other forms of interaction. Thus, when market interactions begin to inflate wage rates, we replace those interactions not with PSI or any other analytical method of wage determination but with the interactions of tripartite bargaining among

---

6. And, of course, to the extent that the rules established were established by prior analysis, the prior analysis was probably casual—drawing on ordinary knowledge—rather than PSI.

representatives of management, labor and the public.

Some forms of interactive problem solving are sometimes disguised as analytical. Among these, perhaps the most common is the delegation of decision making to one or a few persons. In the simplest forms of delegation, the interactive character of problem solving remains clear. If, for example, a group of people, having decided to dine together, have difficulty deciding on a restaurant, they can shortcut or bypass an analysis of the available restaurants and of their own preferences simply by the act of delegating the choice to one among them and by his act of choice. That simple method of interaction will achieve a decision, thus solving their problem; the solution requires no analysis. The delegated person can make a choice, if he wishes, impulsively, according to his own preferences, as arbitrarily as he pleases. He may, or course, turn to analysis, just as he may turn to a toss of a coin. In any case, the group has solved its problem with the act of delegation.

The interactive character of social problem solving is, in some eyes, obscured when decisions are delegated to public officials, including legislators. For some people mistakenly assume that the delegation is no more than an assigning of responsibility to specified officials to undertake analytical problem solving. The actual fact is that the officials may or may not try to achieve or be able to achieve analytical solutions. Legislators, for example, are required to achieve decisions by voting, which is an interactive form of decision making to which their own analyses, if they undertake them, are adapted. Even a single policy maker to whom a decision is delegated may make his choice nonanalytically.

Practitioners of PSI know that some kinds of issues have to be settled by the interactions called "politics" rather than by analysis. But how much that simple fact reveals about the limitations of PSI they have not fully explored.

Nor are the many forms of interactive problem solving outside the political arena familiar or yet explored. As a consequence, we believe that the relation of PSI to interactive problem solving is a question rich in implications yet to be studied.

The Variety of Problem-Solving Interactions

The concept of interactive problem solving will be, in some eyes, disturbingly broad; and indeed an early task in research may be to distinguish among various kinds of interaction. For the present, we mean to consider the whole spectrum of human interaction for its problem-solving capacities. We except only one kind of interaction: deliberately cooperative problem solving through thought or analysis, which we subsume under analytic problem solving.

To suggest that the whole range of human interaction needs to be looked at in that light—as providing alternatives to reaching toward solutions to problems through understanding, thought, or analysis—may seem to border on the bizarre. But to acknowledge that coin tossing is a method of problem solving is to admit as problem-solving a form of human behavior far removed from ratiocination. If coin tossing can produce an answer to a practical problem, so can reading the entrails of fowls. So can trial by water or fire. So can the establishment of routines for action that match responses to problems, as in fire drills, so that when a certain problem for which the routine was established actually arises and there may be no time to think, then the programmed action is a substitute for further analysis.

We have perhaps said enough to discredit the unacceptable notion that interactive methods are primitive, all to be replaced by rational, reasoned, or analyzed problem solving in a more ideal world. Reading the entrails of fowls may be primitive, but markets, voting, and many forms of political bargaining are not.

One has to approach the problem-solving capacities of interaction with considerable openness. Even so, it will be some time, we suggest, before great clarity is achieved. If market interactions are problem solving in that they eventuate in a distribution of income that would otherwise have to be analyzed through to a decision (and then, of course, implemented), what of those interactions called pickpocketing, shoplifting, and holdups? We have already noted that some severe critics of the social order do indeed hold that such interactions actually help solve the problem of inequality by shifting income toward the poor. Similarly, Robin Hood's depredations are argued to have been a form of problem solving for the disadvantaged of his time and vicinity. Numerous forms of human interaction, including many deplored by some people, have, in the eyes of other people, the effect of reducing a social problem, thus achieving an improved outcome. They are thus alternatives to understanding, thought, or analysis as a method of reaching a "solution" or a desired improved outcome. And society—or, specifically, policy makers in any society—always have a choice between trying to find "solutions" (or preferred outcomes) by arranging to have a given problem frontally attacked by persons who will think it through to a solution, or by arranging to set in motion interaction that will, with the help of analysis adapted to the interaction, eventuate in a solution or preferred outcome. Needing investigation are those forms of interaction that serve some significant problem-solving function in society, as, for example, voting, delegation, some forms of political negotiation, and market interactions do, even if some people may see the same interactions as creating problems, as is again the case with voting and markets.

What often obscures our appreciation of interaction as a method of problem solving is that interaction often—perhaps typically—produces both outcome and implementation together, as in resolving the problem of resource allocation and implementing it through the interactions of buying and selling. The problem-solving capacity of interactions is also obscured because the interactions often do not result in a decision by an official or collective authority explicitly resolving a recognized problem. Resource allocation by buying and selling requires no decision *about resource allocation* by anyone, nor need anyone articulate the problem of resource allocation or articulate the answer.

Moreover, interactive problem solving is always mixed with some elements of analytical problem solving, and the latter can take the form of ordinary analysis by problem solvers or the form of PSI either by staff attached to some of many participating problem solvers or by pPSI at a distance, working on their own. The resultant apparent confusion of influence that eventually shapes outcomes discourages pPSI as observers from trying to unravel the process with care, which they could do only by distinguishing precisely between the interactive elements of various kinds and the analytic elements of various kinds and by noting their specific interrelationships. It is the interrelationship of interaction to analysis that is of the greatest significance for PSI.

As we have used it in these pages, the word *solve* may be troublesome. We have already noted (in the preceding chapter) that by problem solving we refer to processes for moving toward a solution. We do not mean that problem solving necessarily wholly solves a problem. In fact, our assumption is that it rarely or never does. Even with that qualification, it might be argued that market interactions do not *solve* the problem of resource allocation; instead they simply bring about an outcome that renders it not a "problem." Fortunately, we do not need to dispute the meaning of the word. Our point is that interactions are a commonly available means of taking some of the steps from here to a better there. In many circumstances, interactions can do what analysis can do, and often they can do what analysis tries but fails to do. Interaction and analysis are alternatives open to society, to its problem solvers, to its policy makers. A choice between them is possible in the same way that one can choose a plane or a train to get to a destination. They are also alternative ways of failing to get from here to a better there, just as both planes and trains sometimes break down.

Complementary Relation Between Analysis and Interaction

We have attached great importance to the fact that analysis and interaction complement each other, as well as compete. They appear in tandem. People engaged in interactions do not stop thinking. Analysis is never wholly turned off. Before tossing a coin, a person may think through the question of whether he ought to toss a coin. To establish an action routine to cope with some kinds of problems, as in the fire-drill example, may require a good deal of analysis in devising an efficient routine. Economists endlessly analyze market structure to see whether market interactions work well or can be made to work better. Yet at some point the coin tosser relies on the toss rather than further analysis. And all the thought that goes into designing a fire drill makes it possible for many persons, when a fire breaks out, to solve the problem of quick escape from a burning building without having to think the problem through at the time. And markets are indeed a substitute for analytical planning of resource allocation even if economists think about and analyze the adequacy of market interactions. Problem-solving interactions change what has to be thought about, what has to be analyzed. In addition, they reduce the amount of thinking that has to be done, the analytical tasks that have to be performed.

It is not true, moreover, that interactive processes, when they are turned to, must be weighed and chosen through analysis. If I am choosing between solving a problem by tossing a coin or by analyzing the problem, I can make that choice by tossing a coin. But how to decide whether to do so? Tossing a coin is always one possible method. There seems to be a possibility for infinite regress. The point, however, is simple: in many cases a solution to a problem can be found either analytically or interactively. Settling on one or the other of the two courses can also be done either through analysis or interaction, and so on. Settling on one or the other is often accomplished through habit, tradition, customs, or routines, rather than explicit analysis of the problem of choice.

How much thought is required to establish interactive problem solving varies from situation to situation. The fire drill requires a good deal, coin tossing little or none. Some interaction we think of as spontaneous and without forethought. An example is the spontaneous evacuation of a building in the absence of a preestablished routine for evacuation. Often that solves the evacuation problem as well as an analyzed decision about an evacuation plan. The one problem-solving method works well daily at 5 P.M.; the other appears to work better in case of fire.

The common declaration that analysis of social problems and of their possible solutions must always be placed in a political or social context, is often merely a pious reminder that pPSI must respect the complexity of the social world. Even when it is more bravely asserted, it is often thin, lacking in substance, since it merely points to interconnections between analysis and other unspecified processes. Our argument that analysis and interaction are both competitive with and complementary to each other as methods for social problem solving begins to pump some substance into the otherwise often weak proposition. Analysis is not simply to be undertaken against a background of political and social processes. Analysis and the other social processes both carry the burden of problem solving for society, and society chooses among various combinations of the two.

Another Concept of Interaction

In suggesting that analytical and interactive problem solving are key categories for research on problem solving, we take note of another fruitful categorization with which it might easily be confused. Weiss has suggested a threefold distinction or, more specifically, three models of the process by which PSI enters into social problem solving.

1. The decision-driven model, in which PSI responds to a problem largely posed by decision makers.
2. The knowledge-driven model, in which "research has thrown up an opportunity that can be capitalized on."
3. The interactive model, in which PSI "is a part of a complex search for knowledge from a variety of sources."[7]

Clearly, all three are models of analytic problem solving, since the models refer to alternative ways of bringing knowledge to bear. What we call interactive problem solving identifies action and interaction as alternatives to knowledge.

7. Carol H. Weiss, Introduction, in Weiss, ed., *Using Social Research in Public Policy Making*, pp. 11–15.

3. Evidence of Misperception

However acceptable and familiar the characterization of routes to social problem solving alternative to PSI just offered, its significance for our purposes is, we suggest, that it is widely denied. Especially in unspoken working assumptions do many—perhaps most—pPSI appear to reveal a misperception of PSI in their rejection of part or all of the characterization. The depth and frequency of that misperception are worth extended investigation.

ANALYSIS VERSUS INTERACTION

One piece of evidence of misperception is the widespread identification of problem solving with problem understanding, to the exclusion of interaction. For example, a political scientist writes: "The solution of societal problems generally implies a rational model." And he specifies that a rational model "requires complete understanding."[1] We suspect that in one part of their minds many pPSI take it for granted that the normal or necessary way to solve any problem is to understand it. They do not systematically conceive of problem solving as other than an intellectual or cognitive process, any more than they can conceive of rationality except by reference to intellectual or cognitive processes. Thus, in many of their systematic formulations of conceptions of problem solving, as well as in their choice of direction for research, they ignore the possibility of interactive problem solving. Although in another part of their minds they cannot deny that "politics" as one form of interactive problem solving is often a necessary element in problem solving, they nevertheless recommend the ap-

1. Thomas Dye, *Understanding Public Policy*, 2d ed. (Englewood Cliffs, N.J.: Prentice-Hall, 1975), pp. 27 and 344.

plication of PSI to all important social problems as though interactive solutions were not worth considering as an alternative.

Here, for example, appears to be a categorical denial of the possibility of interactive problem solving, except, perhaps, as an aberration: "no sensible policy choice can be made without careful analysis of the advantages and disadvantages of each course of action."[2] For another example: "The distinctive quality of social policy is its aim for what might be called programmatic rationality; it seeks to achieve substantive goals through instrumental action programs *that can be proven logically or empirically*, to achieve these goals."[3]

There is nothing unusual about these statements. We do not single them out for their conspicuousness. Similar statements abound in the literature of social science and social research. They all seem to deny—sometimes flatly and without ambiguity—the frequency with which interactions solve problems without anyone's understanding or analysis.

Commenting on over forty contributors to *The Uses of Sociology*, its editors note: "There is agreement that policy should be *evaluated*. . . ."[4] We suspect that most pPSI would agree—thus universally prescribing analytical problem solving to the neglect of interactive problem solving. Yet they would also, if pressed, quickly abandon the proposition. They carry an inconsistency in their minds that misguides PSI.

We further suggest that, economists aside, those pPSI

2. Edith Stokey and Richard Zeckhauser, *A Primer for Policy Analysis* (New York: Norton, 1978), p. ix.

3. Herbert J. Gans, "Social Science for Social Policy," in Irving Louis Horowitz, ed., *The Use and Abuse of Social Science*, 2d ed. (New Brunswick, N.J.: Transaction Books, 1975), p. 4. Our italics.

4. Paul F. Lazarsfeld, William H. Sewell, and Harold L. Wilensky, eds., *The Uses of Sociology*, p. xv.

who grasp analytic problem solving as one alternative and interactive as another, frequently neglect all forms of interaction except politics. A more generalized perception, vision, or model of interactive problem solving is, we think, not to be found in the literature of problem solving and policy making.[5] It would include political, market, and other subtle forms so far only dimly perceived—for example, those interactions that largely solve the problem posed by the question: "What basic moral rules should be established to maintain social peace?"

Even political interaction does not seem to be clearly or fully perceived as a form of problem solving. Practitioners of PSI record their regret over its obstruction to rational problem solving far more often than their appreciation of it as a method of problem solving. We take as an example an article on social science contributions to health policy. It is noted that interest groups interact on health policy. It is further noted that they are frequently obstructive (as indeed they often are). The author then goes on to note that interest groups can make a positive contribution to problem solving if those officials and scholars who best know what needs to be done can mobilize them for support. That their interactions themselves ever constitute a problem-solving process alternative to PSI or other analytic problem solving is entirely overlooked.[6]

Even in an unusual explicit attempt to clarify the relation of analytical problem solving to political problem solving, Charles Schultze sees little more in interactive problem solving than what he calls adversary bargaining or "politi-

5. A beginning may be found in Charles E. Lindblom, "The Sociology of Planning: Thought and Interaction," in Morris Bornstein, ed, *Economic Planning: East and West* (Cambridge, Mass.: Ballinger, 1975) and in somewhat revised form in Charles E. Lindblom, *Politics and Markets* (New York: Basic Books, 1977), chaps. 19 and 23.

6. Edward A. Suchman, "Public Health" in Lazarsfeld, Sewell, and Wilensky, *Uses of Sociology*, pp. 583–84.

cal dialogue,'' thus denying by implication—or simply missing the fact—that many other forms of interaction contribute to problem solving both in and outside the political arena.[7] It is probably correct to suggest that generally among pPSI what we call interactive problem solving in the political arena is often reduced in concept to only one of its forms, bargaining, to the exclusion of tacit reciprocity, preemption, deference to adversaries, and forms of mutual adjustment at a distance in which the parties need not communicate with each other.[8]

Presumption of ''The Decision Maker''

Another evidence of pPSI misperception is indirect. In interactive problem solving, a given problem is usually ameliorated or solved other than by some person's specific decision governing or encompassing that problem. Sometimes, of course, an interactive process will eventuate in a decision that can be attributed to an official or committee; but often not. Instead the outcome will emerge from such interactions as, for example, when a price is established in a competitive market without anyone's playing the role of price setter. The price is more a happening than any one person's decision to establish it, even if thousands of buying and selling decisions led to the result. If, then, pPSI fall into the habit of presuming an identifiable decision maker on each problem, his decision somehow encompassing and governing the outcome, we take as evidence that they do not understand the possibilities of interactive problem solving and are therefore likely to misperceive the role of PSI and other analytical methods because they misperceive its audiences as ''the decision maker.''

Just such a presumption is common, though not univer-

7. Charles Schultze, *The Politics and Economics of Public Spending* (Washington, D.C.: Brookings Institution, 1968), esp. pp. 77 and 92.
8. For a list, see Charles E. Lindblom, *The Intelligence of Democracy* (New York: Free Press, 1965), pt. 2, esp. p. 84.

sal; and we shall give examples. The presumption is all the more interesting when entertained by pPSI who know better. For instance, the authors of a recent study of difficulties in public policy making explicitly indicate that they understand that policy often emerges from a welter of conflicting influences, including those in which none or only a few of the various participants openly face and acknowledge responsibility for attacking the ostensible problem. That is, they acknowledge the common situation in which an outcome will emerge from interaction among decision makers, each of whom is in pursuit of solutions to his own problems rather than the ostensible problem. But the authors then simply set this perception aside and propose instead to examine policy making as though it were accomplished exclusively by identifiable decision makers with assigned responsibilities for a given problem who attack the ostensible problem with appropriate criteria for its solution. Thus, they write:

> We examine policy making from the perspective of the decision makers, scrutinizing the intellectual tasks facing those who must both make policy decisions and see that they are implemented. On what are they to base their decisions? What criteria are they to use to choose between alternatives?[9]

These are questions, we suggest, appropriate to a view of problem solving as analytic, one that excludes interaction.

Another example shows how interactive problem solving is simply ignored. In this case, at least one form of it is acknowledged to exist but is excluded from study, apparently because it is too difficult to handle. "We will not consider," the authors write, "the situations in which several decision makers with conflicting objectives participate

9. George C. Edwards III and Ira Sharkansky, *The Policy Predicament* (San Francisco: W. H. Freeman, 1978), p. 5.

in a decision.'' Nor, will they consider, apparently, those even more complex interactions in which an outcome is achieved without even a group decision on it. As a result, their approach to policy analysis is ''that of the rational decision maker who lays out goals and uses logical processes to explore the best way to reach those goals.''[10]

This is a drastically simplified picture of policy making and has the effect, we suggest, of perpetuating the identification of problem solving with problem understanding to the exclusion of problem-solving interaction. It seriously distorts the role of analysis in problem solving, because it ignores the complex interactive process in which analysis must ordinarily be relevant—often in varied ways—to the actions of many problem solvers. Looking only at *a* or *the* decision maker may artificially enhance or reduce our estimates of the importance of analysis.

THE PSI RELATION TO ORDINARY KNOWLEDGE

On the inability of PSI to achieve more than a supplement to ordinary knowledge, the evidence of misperception by pPSI is for the most part indicated by silence on the subject. There is little evidence that the relation between the two is much investigated. Instead, there is a tendency to distinguish too sharply between social scientific and ordinary knowledge. For example, pPSI are characterized by one of them as aspiring to be ''unswayed by unsubstantiated opinion'' despite, if we are correct, the certainty that all pPSI are necessarily so swayed, dependent as they must be on ordinary knowledge.[11] In any case, PSI is repeatedly presented as highly distinctive, as offering something unique to social problem solving—offerings that cannot be reconciled with the characterization of PSI laid out in the immediately preceding chapter.

10. Stokey and Zeckhauser, *Primer for Policy Analysis*, p. 3.
11. John E. Brandl, ''Evaluation and Politics,'' *Evaluation* (Special Issue, 1978), p. 6.

Another example is a series of five essays solicited by the editor of the *American Journal of Political Science* to clarify policy analysis and its functions. In each of them, knowledge is identified with professional and scientific knowledge, and no significant reference is made to any other forms or sources of knowledge.[12] For another example, in the introduction of *The Uses of Sociology*, the editors add to their observation that policy should be evaluated, the categorical statement that "the social scientist is the proper man to provide the information."[13] That there are other appropriate sources of information—the expertise of the administrator, for example, or journalism—and that PSI might therefore best be specialized to provide inputs that alternative sources cannot well provide, does not appear to occur to them.

Nor does Schultze's argument for more analysis and less bargaining in public policy, referred to above, raise significant questions about the relation of PSI to ordinary knowledge. His case for more carefully analyzed policies is entirely a case for PSI, to the exclusion of such other sources as journalism, expertise acquired on the job, and information generated by collegial reflection on the job and its problems. Schultze acknowledges that not all policy problems can be professionally analyzed and that policy makers will have to employ their own quick and superficial analyses for most of their problems. But questions about when PSI should be drawn on and when not do not engage him. Nor does the attempt to specify the distinctive advantages of PSI over ordinary information and analysis from other sources challenge him. And clearly the possibility that much of PSI is itself quick and superficial does not much qualify his broad endorsement of it.

12. Essays were submitted by Martin Landau, Heinz Eulau, David B. Brobrow, Charles O. Jones, and Robert Axelrod, *American Journal of Political Science*, vol. 21 (May 1977).
13. Lazarsfeld, Sewell, and Wilensky, *Uses of Sociology*, p. xv.

The neglect of ordinary knowledge in analyses of an appropriate role for PSI may have its origins in intellectual traditions in science and in the philosophy of science, in which a role for ordinary knowledge is also frequently neglected. An example may be Ernest Nagel's *Structure of Science*.[14] It opens with an analysis of differences between ordinary and scientific knowledge, and it is thus immediately brought to our attention that Nagel is fully aware of a vast body of ordinary knowledge. But typical of many expositions of scientific method, Nagel does not investigate possible complementary relations between the two forms of knowledge. Specifically, he does not even ask whether aspirations toward greater scientific knowledge might best envision scientific knowledge as a supplement to ordinary knowledge rather than a replacement for it.

IMPERIAL PSI

A few citations illuminate the carelessness, professional bias, or audaciousness with which both interactive and analytic alternatives to PSI are deprecated or simply ignored. "From one point of view," writes one social scientist, "the principal strategy of the policy sciences can be summed up as guiding the focus of attention of all participants in decision."[15] A student of the philosophy of social science writes: "The behavioral scientist would do well to remember that when science is divorced from policy, the result is not only that science is 'set free' but also that policy is thereby thrown on its own resources— which is to say that it is left to be determined by tradition, prejudice, and the preponderance of power."[16]

14. Ernest Nagel, *Structure of Science* (New York: Harcourt, Brace and World, 1971).

15 Harold D. Lasswell, *A Pre-View of Policy Sciences* (New York: American Elsevier, 1971), p. 61.

16. Abraham Kaplan, *The Conduct of Inquiry* (San Francisco: Chandler Publishing Co., 1964), p. 61.

A political scientist declares that for coping with difficult social problems, social science is "the only technology that government has at hand."[17] Even the confident conventional view that the function of social scientists is to move toward "a greater body of scientifically valid knowledge"[18] is careless in ignoring the possibility that PSI may be forever destined to do no more than reshape and refine ordinary knowledge.

The misperception by its practitioners of the relation of PSI to other analytical and to interactive inputs into social problem solving is, it may have been noticed in some of our examples of it, attested less by their explicit error than by their neglect of other inputs when they contemplate the proper role for PSI in social problem solving. A final example is Dror's *Public Policymaking Reexamined*.[19]

Dror is aware of the full range of analytical inputs, of which PSI is only one or one category. Yet he formulates the problem of improving the policy-making process in such a way as to turn him away from considering how the PSI input relates to the other inputs. His diagnosis of the policy-making process treats policy making almost entirely as an intellectual problem, to the near exclusion of interactive problem solving, as is indicated by his summary evaluation of policy making in his chapter 11. And, even if we accept his considered judgment that new inputs of information and analysis constitute the main road to reform, we note that he slides from the need for more knowledge and analysis to the need for more social scien-

17. Richard Rose, "Disciplined Research and Undisciplined Problems," in Carol H. Weiss, ed. *Using Social Research in Public Policy Making*, p. 35.

18. Rensis Likert and Ronald Lippit, "The Utilization of Social Science," in Leon Festinger and Daniel Katz, *Research Methods in the Behavioral Sciences* (New York: Dryden, 1953), p. 581.

19. Yehezkel Dror, *Public Policymaking Reexamined* (San Francisco: Chandler Publishing Co., 1968).

tific knowledge and analysis (chapter 1), as though ordinary knowledge and analysis are not worth further discussion. This neglect of interaction and of ordinary knowledge is not unimportant; it powerfully affects his recommendations for improving policy making, specifically loading onto PSI burdens it may not be able to carry. For if in fact it is always only a supplement to ordinary knowledge, then great care is needed in expanding the tasks of PSI lest it be hopelessly overextended.

4. The Mistaken Pursuit of Authoritativeness

Misperception by its practitioners of the relation of PSI to other inputs into social problem solving results in a variety of research practices that are either questionable or mistaken. It thus also has implications for improved PSI practices. We have yet to spell out both the dubious practices and the implied improvements, although we have already mentioned a number of them.

Before we move on to them in chapter 5, we need to examine certain other misunderstandings about PSI widely shared by its practitioners. In this examination, the central question can be formulated as one concerning the authoritativeness of PSI. We suggest that it is not, and cannot be, as authoritative as many pPSI believe it is or might become.

The issue of authoritativeness arises in the following way. If we want to explain—asking why—the limited role that PSI plays alongside ordinary knowledge, social learning, and interactive problem solving, two points immediately spring to mind. First, PSI is costly, so much so that it cannot be used for most social problems nor pushed to conclusive answers on those issues on which it is used. Second, even if it were a free good, and thus available without constraint of manpower, materials, or money, it cannot achieve scientifically definitive or conclusive answers on certain kinds of questions. At core, both of these explanations trace to the complexity of the social world and, in the face of that complexity, man's limited cognitive capacity. To stretch that capacity is enormously costly; and even if it were stretched as far as imaginable, it could not handle certain kinds of questions.

At least some of the implications of the costliness of PSI

The Mistaken Pursuit of Authoritativeness 41

for good practice are obvious. Since PSI cannot cover the whole terrain of problems to be solved, good practice requires discrimination in what is attempted. The difficulty of finding funds to support their research requires pPSI to give at least some attention to cost. Even the most apparent implications of cost for good practice are, however, often missed, as when, for example, it is recommended that "the level of spending on basic research should be such as to allow funding of all meritorious research proposals," a prescription that recommends the impossible.[1]

Implications of costs for the conclusiveness with which PSI can establish propositions on those questions it attacks, pose more difficult and interesting issues. They intertwine, however, with other issues that also concern the conclusiveness of PSI propositions—specifically, those arising out of PSI incapacities other than its costliness.

To clarify the main issues bearing on the inconclusiveness (for whatever reason) of PSI propositions is, thus, to illuminate causes of and implications of misperceptions about the relation of PSI to other inputs into social problem solving. But the inconclusiveness of PSI is itself— independent of its connection with the preceding chapters—a major issue. Independently, we suggest, overestimating PSI's conclusiveness accounts for serious failures and flaws in the practice of PSI and points toward desirable new practices.

For our purpose—which is that of developing issues bearing on the usefulness of PSI in social problem solving—the conclusiveness issue needs to be somewhat amended. PSI knowledge might be scientifically conclusive—or reasonably so—yet for some other reason be rejected for social problem solving. Let us therefore distinguish between the question of whether a proposition is

1. National Academy of Sciences, *Basic Research and National Goals* (U.S. House of Representatives Committee Print, Committee on Science and Astronautics, March 1965), p. 276.

reasonably verified scientifically and the question of whether anyone will act on the belief or assumption that it is true. PSI might establish as scientifically highly verified the proposition that children learn as well in large classes as in small ones, yet no school superintendent might be willing to act on such a conclusive finding, even though he knows of it, in agitating for new policies, in establishing class sizes in his schools, or in advising parents on the educational needs of their children. He may be skeptical or hostile to it for many reasons. If he is not willing to accept it, we shall say that, however conclusive the knowledge is by scientific standards, it is not *authoritative* for him. It does not, in his eyes, warrant his acting on it.

Conclusiveness is necessary but not sufficient for authoritativeness.[2] Moreover, since scientific conclusiveness is a matter of degree, so also is authoritativeness. And authoritativeness of knowledge, we suggest, varies from person to person even more than judgments of conclusiveness.

We also need to distinguish between two kinds of authoritativeness, or two ways in which it can at least hypothetically be achieved. In the first case, a proposition is authoritative because its degree of scientific conclusiveness is high (and there are no positive obstructions to its authoritativeness on other grounds). In the second case, it is authoritative because, although its scientific conclusive-

---

2. Some knowledge (including misinformation) for some people under some circumstances is decisive even though it is without a shred of scientific confirmation. That is to say, it is in their eyes sufficient basis for action; it warrants their acting on it. You make your plans for the day on the supposition that it is Tuesday, a belief you hardly need to subject to scientific testing. But pPSI are not greatly concerned with decisiveness as just defined. They wish to develop knowledge that warrants action because of its scientific conclusiveness, because of the professional care that has gone into discovering and confirming it. It is this quality that we wish to capture in the idea of authoritative knowledge: knowledge that serves as a basis for commitment or action because it has met to a significant degree professional standards for verification.

ness leaves a good deal to be desired, the scientific or professional tests confirm or are confirmed by ordinary knowledge (fallible as both may be). In the second case, PSI achieves a sufficient degree of conclusiveness to make the knowledge authoritative, but only because PSI adds to the weight of ordinary knowledge. In the first case, we shall say that PSI is independently authoritative; in the second case, dependently authoritative.

Some pPSI may be disturbed at the thought that ordinary knowledge can confirm PSI knowledge or that it is appropriate to think of so powerful an instrument as PSI being cast in the role of confirming ordinary knowledge. Yet in fact PSI knowledge is often less conclusive than ordinary knowledge. That increased market demand usually means higher prices, that war will occur again somewhere in the world, that decades from now some people will still live in poverty, that newly invented technologies will on some counts greatly raise our standard of living in the future, that political democracy will arise in some nations and vanish from others within the next generation—all are more conclusive propositions for social problem solving than most formally tested propositions of PSI. Indeed, most ostensible scientific PSI propositions, such as those statistically tested at great expense in the controversies over the educational consequences of school desegregation, are extremely shaky and widely challenged as soon as first asserted.

MISPERCEPTIONS

With these distinctions, we now suggest that its practitioners frequently misperceive PSI. They mistakenly believe: that pPSI should strive for independent authoritativeness; that pPSI should above all strive for the scientific conclusiveness that is necessary to authoritativeness, with little attention to the other requirements for authoritativeness; and that there is no other significant role for PSI than the attainment of authoritativeness.

The contrary views we suggest are: that PSI can ordinarily not be independently authoritative; that pPSI would be more effective if they were to strive only for dependent authoritativeness; that for dependent authoritativeness their achievement of a high degree of scientific conclusiveness, even where it is possible, is not enough (since in addition PSI has to be confirmed by ordinary knowledge); that pPSI must consequently always attend in addition to the relation between their knowledge and the ordinary knowledge that confirms it; and that, finally, there are in any case alternative roles for PSI that do not require authoritativeness, either independent or dependent.

In this chapter, we go no further than to indicate why PSI cannot usually be independently authoritative. And why it should then discriminatingly pursue no more than dependent authority. In chapter 6, we shall indicate how the misperception diverts PSI into inappropriate work and ways in which PSI can be useful without being authoritative.

The misperceptions, we suggest, arise from a traditional deeply rooted belief that scientific inquiry is the pursuit of verified propositions. Science is, in such a view, the pursuit of truth, a method of eliminating false opinion, a way to perceive reality correctly. Even if they allow for persistent error and long-standing differences in findings, most scientists and pPSI find it difficult to conceive of science and professional investigation as other than a process that ultimately moves toward convergence on propositions, toward an increasingly correct representation of reality.[3] All these notions seem to imply that pPSI should pursue confirmed knowledge or scientific conclusiveness. And

3. For various views of science that share such a conception, see M. J. Mulkay, "Three Models of Scientific Development," *Sociological Review* 23 (August 1975): 509–13, and 521. See also S. White and M. Rein, "Can Research Help Policy?" *Public Interest* 44 (Fall 1977): 134–35.

from the aspiration to achieve scientific conclusiveness, it is assumed that one can take a quick, short jump to authoritativeness.

FAILURES OF AUTHORITATIVENESS

That these are indeed fundamental misconceptions will become clearer if we look at various aspects of the failures of authoritativeness, beginning with some that can be passed over quickly because of their familiarity.

Nonrational Responses to PSI

Perhaps the most familiar failures to achieve authoritativeness of either kind (and for that reason the least interesting for present purposes) stem from many irrational and nonrational human resistances to believing what pPSI, or scientists generally, say. The skepticism or hostility of the government official toward the professional researcher, for example, is much commented upon. So also is his reluctance, for many irrational and nonrational reasons, to take the trouble to digest PSI knowledge even when it is made easily available to him. All these familiar considerations bearing on authoritativeness we pass over, not because they lack importance but because they are already widely identified and their implications for the practice of PSI much discussed. Their general tenor is to lay blame on users of PSI and to suggest how the practice of PSI, especially the presentation of its results to potential users, has to be adapted to the shortcomings of the users.

PSI Incompetence on Normative Issues

We are more interested in pointing up failures of authoritativeness that arise out of problem complexity and PSI inconclusiveness in the face of complexity. Of these, one is again sufficiently familiar to warrant only the briefest attention. That is the alleged incompetence of scientific inquiry to settle the value or normative questions that always arise in social problem solving. According to this allegation, PSI cannot even go so far as to achieve scientific conclusiveness or any approximation to it on normative questions, and instead remains silent on those issues. That being so, it can hardly be authoritative on them.

The allegation, if true, throws light immediately on one of the many reasons why people inescapably turn to ordinary knowledge and why, alternatively, many normative issues are thrown into the arena for interactive rather than analytic settlement.

The allegation is not entirely true. Ostensibly normative analysis, we suggest, is overwhelmingly empirical in form. That is, social scientists, philosophers, and other people typically argue about values and norms by making statements most of which are, in principle, factual.[4] An objection, for example, to higher taxes is that they will impede business incentives, which is a statement factual in form. Evaluative discourse thus appears to be open to the contribution of PSI; and pPSI are misdirected when, as is often the case, they permit a misconception on the point to direct them away from normative issues.

But the allegation is not entirely false either. We do not challenge the widespread opinion among pPSI that not all normative propositions can be translated into empirical ones, that one is eventually driven back to end-of-the-line propositions that have to be treated as axioms, or as articles of faith, or as expressions of preference or emotion. Clearly, then, as is well recognized, even if PSI is scientifically conclusive on its empirical propositions, it cannot

---

4. Almost any book or article on a policy issue seems to serve as evidence of the truth of the hypothesis. But for one example, see the empirical character of various arguments over public policy toward labor unions in municipal public employment in H. H. Wellington and R. K. Winter, Jr., *The Unions and the Cities* (Washington, D.C.: Brookings Institution, 1971).

achieve authoritativeness for action without normative propositions that lie beyond its competence to establish.[5]

Divergence

Much less familiar an obstacle to authoritativeness—specifically to independent authoritativeness—is one that goes to the very foundations of social science and PSI. Standing in sharp contrast to the customary belief in the tendency of scientific investigation to converge on increasingly correct representations of reality is the phenomenon of divergence that marks much of social science and PSI. Examples abound. Commenting on fifteen years of PSI analysis of productivity, profits, and living costs designed, at least in part, to illuminate policy on wage inflation and unemployment, John Dunlop, economist and former U.S. Secretary of Labor notes: "Some analysts have concluded the relation among these variables to be strong, others that it has been quite weak; some hold that wage responses to increasing unemployment are moderate

---

5. Practitioners of PSI sometimes suggest that, if their clients provide them with the required normative propositions—that is, their values—then PSI can proceed to authoritative conclusions. In that simple faith lie several issues that need unraveling. The clients are often, of course, multiple and are in disagreement on values. The client also often explicitly or implicitly asks the pPSI for advice on values and cannot tell the pPSI what values to take as given. Even if the client is single and is willing to declare his own values, subsequent policy recommendations made by the pPSI will not be authoritative for any persons whose values are different.

Perhaps most important to signaling issues that call for intense further study, it appears to be impossible to articulate values with any precision prior to empirical analysis of issues to which the values are relevant. To tell, for example, a pPSI that he should take full employment to be an important value when he analyzes and appraises fiscal policy, does not tell him how important it is relative to other relevant values like price stability or low taxes. Nor does it tell him whether it is to be regarded as more important than other values that he will discover to be relevant only as his empirical analysis proceeds. It does not, in short, tell him what the schedule of trade-offs should be between full employment and ever-emerging other values at issue.

while others hold that wage responses are becoming more inflationary. . . .''[6]

Our ignorance grows, as Popper has observed, along with our knowledge. Or, in the words of another, "the outcome of any serious research can only be to make two questions grow where one question grew before."[7] We suggest that the usual effect of PSI is to raise new issues, stimulate new debate, and multiply the complexities of the social problem at hand.

Divergence can, of course, be passed off as transitory, in which case it does not challenge the widespread faith in the power of PSI finally to reach agreed propositions. Yet it appears that in many fields the increase in conflict over issues is not transitory but remains or even grows as PSI continues to uncover even more complex aspects of reality.[8] Research on social stratification and school busing illustrates the indefinite proliferation of diverse issues, findings, and hypotheses, rather than convergence.

Although the question of divergence can be posed with brevity, its significance for social science and PSI is enormous. The frequency of divergence rather than convergence will open up in some minds the possibility that, whenever it is divergent, hence not conclusive, and hence not authoritative, PSI in fact has no important contribution to make to social problem solving. In chapter 6 we shall examine a more reasonable inference to be explored: that PSI makes its contribution, despite its muddying of waters, in ways other than those leading to independent authoritativeness via convergence of opinion. In any case, questions

6. John T. Dunlop, "Policy Decisions and Research in Economic and Industrial Relations," *Industrial and Labor Relations Review* 30 (April 1977).

7. Thorstein Veblen, *The Place of Science in Modern Civilization* (New York: Russell and Russell Publishers, 1961), p. 33.

8. The issue is posed by David Cohen and Janet Weiss, "Social Science and Social Policy: Schools and Race," *The Educational Forum* 41 (May 1977): 393–413.

have to be asked: Under what circumstances does PSI move toward divergence? In what specific ways might PSI be valuable despite divergence? What kinds of PSI best take advantage of those ways?

In the face of divergence of scientific findings, although independent PSI authoritativeness becomes impossible, it seems clear that dependent authoritativeness remains possible. One of the divergent views (which like its rivals enjoys some degree of scientific confirmation) confirms or is confirmed by some people's ordinary knowledge. They then take that view as authoritative, thus act on it. It appears that a great deal of PSI offered to problem solvers is of just this kind.

Defining, Bounding, or Constructing Problems

A common failure to achieve an authoritative solution to a problem arises because critics or skeptics of the solution easily can—and do—allege that the problem has been incorrectly defined.

Suppose we begin, as an exercise in defining a problem, with the familiar "Why Johnny can't read." To specify the problem more precisely, someone will suggest that the problem is one of reading difficulties among certain urban ethnic groups. But then it will be said that the problem is one of inadequate family incomes for these groups. And to that it will be responded that income itself is not the problem; the problem is basically a deficiency in the family's ability to implant an incentive to learn to read in children. Hence the problem becomes that of the inadequacy of the urban ethnic family as a social institution—an institution that is failing to perform its required functions. That may provoke the suggestion that the problem is one of defective socioeconomic organization; socioeconomic institutions do not integrate these families into normal social functioning. But perhaps, then, the problem is one of faulty political organization in the society at large, since presumably the right kind of political decision could remedy the faults of the economy, the structure of urban society, and the place of the family in it.

At this point someone is also certain to suggest that politics is not an independent influence on economy and society, being itself dependent upon them. It might then be proposed that the problem is one big interlocked problem of social organization—to which formulation one may or may not add some further problem specification, such as that the phenomena of social class are the "real" problem. But problem definition at this level can perhaps be counted on to produce another abstract formulation. Any big inter- locked problem of social organization, it will be suggested, can only be understood as a product of history and culture. The problem, then, is a fundamental one of a historically produced culture that is inadequate. From which it seems only a small step to the conclusion: the world is not what it should be. That is the problem.

Of all these attempts to define *the* or *a* problem, none is correct (or incorrect). The notion of an authoritative PSI is therefore strained. We do not discover a problem "out there"; we make a choice about how we want to formulate a problem. And, of course, opinions will also differ as to whether a *phenomenon* is or is not a *problem*. War is often taken to be a problem, yet nations use war as a solution to problems. And is decline of parental authority a problem, or an indication of desirable social trend?

Obsolescence of PSI Knowledge

Finally, PSI fails of authoritativeness because, as is familiar, it tries to describe or predict the ever-changing behavior of learning human beings, and it even provides them with learning. From all their experiences and sources of information, human beings learn to behave differently with each passing month or year; and they thus constantly render PSI generalizations about their behavior obsolete.

Contrary to the general assumption that valid scientific knowledge cumulates, much of the mid-twentieth century investment of American political science in survey research on voting, a body of generalization to which the profession pointed with pride when claiming a new scientific status, is already obsolete. There are even signs that some of the general propositions of macrotheory in economics, once among the most secure holdings of social science, have become obsolete in a changing society that now displays inflation and depression simultaneously. (Of course, much of the statistical reporting done by social scientists, social research institutions, and government agencies rapidly becomes obsolete, sometimes even before it can be published, although it remains part of the historical record.)

In some periods of rapid change, it is a possibility—although we do not know how one could firmly establish such a fact—that PSI falls behind; specifically, pPSI lose more knowledge than they gain. And if the common presumption is that PSI produces a cumulation of knowledge, the cumulation may be at best extremely slow.

Commenting on the obsolescence of voting studies, the authors of a recent study write:

> the description of the electoral process of the late fifties no longer holds, and that change in the electoral process came in response to political events. Does this mean that all political processes are contingent on the events of the day and that generalization is impossible about political matters? The electrolysis instruments continue to produce hydrogen and oxygen decade after decade. The survey instruments produce different results now than they did a while back. Nevertheless, we remain convinced that generalization is possible, even

about matters as volatile as politics. But the generalizations will have to take time into account.[9]

In principle, authoritativeness is still possible only if PSI is thus focused on the unchanging aspects of human behavior. But it is the changing aspects that are often pertinent to social problems and their solutions. Businessmen's behavior, not in its unchanging aspects but in its specific 1970s pattern, may be the crucial element in present economic policy. Hence, we suggest, useful PSI is destined for steady obsolescence and on that specific ground in addition to all the others cannot, as a consequence, attain authoritativeness.

PSI knowledge, we have argued, is almost never conclusive, hence for that and other reasons almost never independently authoritative. If the common pPSI aspiration is that PSI become a source of independent authoritative knowledge, the actual fact is that PSI acquires no more than dependent authoritativeness together with other inputs into problem solving. A PSI finding, never itself independently authoritative, will often become authoritative if it confirms ordinary knowledge, and often not if it contradicts it. And, as is familiar, it will become authoritative in some users' minds if it squares with their ideology or conforms to their general world view or epistemological position, but not otherwise.

Hence PSI knowledge is, again, best seen as an increment to other knowledge. Now and then it adds sufficient weight to carry a proposition across the line of disbelief. In presumably rare circumstances, it issues an outright challenge to a substantial body of established belief. In these circumstances, however, it probably achieves its impact on

9. Norman Nie, Sidney Verba, and John Petrocik, *The Changing American Voter* (Cambridge, Mass.: Harvard University Press, 1976), p. 9.

that body because it is an increment to another body of established belief that has been in conflict with the first. In any of these cases, we may be tempted to speak of it as authoritative (hence also conclusive); but, strictly speaking, it is not. It is only when PSI and other knowledge are joined in mutual support that knowledge about the social world becomes authoritative.

If, then, pPSI wish to hold to their traditional aspiration of achieving authoritativeness, we suggest that, they must, again, adapt their work to other inputs into social problem solving in many ways not yet sufficiently explored.

5. Improving the Professional Social Inquiry Relation to Other Inputs

We can now return to certain issues pertaining to the PSI relation to other inputs into social problem solving. If it is true that PSI is only one among several no less important inputs, and if it is also true that many pPSI proceed as though denying so, then it follows, as we suggested earlier, that pPSI will indiscriminately attempt too many tasks rather than selectively choosing critical supplements or complementarities to the other inputs; will spend their energies on tasks they cannot do well, as well as on those they need not do; and will fail to focus on tasks they can do. These general inferences were apparent in the arguments of chapters 2 and 3, and we shall here carry our search for inferences a little further.

SOME ILLUSTRATIVE IMPLICATIONS

For our present purposes, it would be tedious to spell all these inferences out in great detail. It is already clear, we trust, that the argument that has predicted misdirection of PSI needs to be given further analysis and empirical testing and that study can further specify both the consequences and their implications for redirection of PSI.

Some of the implications for PSI redirection are not easy to accept—or even to consider thoughtfully. If, for example, ordinary knowledge is superior to PSI on some issues, it may be prudent—at least for a long time to come—for pPSI to decide to terminate or drastically curtail PSI on those issues. That is a distasteful decision for pPSI, especially for those specialized in the study of those particular issues. Or, if social learning rather than PSI is called for on some problems, again it may be almost impossible for pPSI to disqualify themselves.

Social Learning and Its Displacement of PSI

It may not be much easier to consider another implication of the need for social learning, one that provides a good example of the redirections of PSI that need to be analyzed for their implications for the practice of PSI. The example is that of the displacement, because of the need for social learning, of one PSI problem by others. When social learning is required, as, for example, on the changes in attitudes required for coping with inflation or energy problems (as discussed in chapter 2), it may be that much inflation and energy research needs to be displaced by research on how to facilitate the required social learning. A problem for PSI, among others, might be to try to find stimuli to the learning of new expectations other than the eventual costly crisis that often finally brings such learning about. Energy specialists will of course resist the suggestion that they may have less to offer about society's energy problems than, say, a social psychologist grappling with problems in social learning.[1]

The merit of the example we have chosen is that it makes the point simply. But it is not a persuasive example because, given the record of PSI, it is difficult to see how PSI can contribute much to the discovery of ways to stimulate social learning of new attitudes or expectations. Indeed, such an assignment might push PSI into just those impossible tasks against which these pages caution.

A better though more complex example is suggested by a few excursions of PSI (in particular, political science) into

---

1. The general public aside, policy makers have a great deal of learning of information and skills required for their specialized roles to do too. Practitioners of PSI often incorrectly assume that policy makers want help from PSI on the substance of policy under their jurisdiction. A study of roughly a hundred different problems facing thirty policy makers disclosed that their PSI needs, in their own eyes, converged on problems in organization and interpersonal relations rather than on the substance of policy. (Hans L. Zetterberg, *Social Theory and Social Practice* [New York: Bedminster, 1962], p. 40).

the role of political leadership in reconstructing popular demands, attitudes, and expectations so that policies that were impossible earlier subsequently become possible. The distinction drawn is between the leader who takes popular preferences or volitions as given, thus developing policies that accommodate them, and the reconstructive leader who reshapes them, thus opening up new opportunities for problem solving.[2]

Our suggestion is that, if the reconstructive leader is sometimes necessary, as he may be for both the inflation and the energy problems, it may be that PSI might more effectively come to his assistance with political studies than to the assistance of, say, the energy administrator with energy studies. Because pPSI are usually locked into their own specialities and are accustomed to frontal attacks on problems, we doubt that they are sufficiently sensitive to the need, from time to time, for drastic displacement of their energies—that is, for drastic redefinition of the problem that needs attention.

Epiphenomenal Problem Solving

Other implications are much easier to accept, but they nonetheless call for substantial improvement in pPSI awareness of problems in selecting research tasks. An example is the adaptation, which is badly done and might be much improved, of PSI to epiphenomenal or by-product problem solving.

We have said that problems are often solved through interaction rather than analysis. There is, however, still another way in which problems are solved without being placed on anyone's analytical agenda. An example will make the point. Domestic politics in the U.S.A. was long marked by two related problems: inadequate party competi-

2. See, for example, Eric Nordlinger, *Conflict Regulation in Divided Societies* (Cambridge, Mass.: Harvard University Center for International Affairs, 1972).

tion in the Southern states and obstructions to legislation posed by the seniority system in Congress. The first problem was then solved to a degree by an invigoration of the Republican Party in the South. As a largely unanticipated result, most senior members of Congressional committees were no longer conservative Southerners who owed their seniority to safe districts (safe because of an absence of party competition). And as a consequence of that, the second problem—the obstructive effect of seniority—was greatly reduced. Solving one problem solved another, epiphenomenally.[3]

We all know that when society tries to solve one problem it often creates others. Our point is simply that, alternatively, when society tries to solve one problem, it often solves others.

Until recently, we "solved" the problem of maintaining the quality of life in America largely by letting its quality emerge from decisions on countless specific matters such as, for example, highway construction, zoning, care of the aged, public education, and economic growth. The implicit issue of quality of life was nowhere raised as a policy question. It was solved epiphenomenally. Many people now want to attack the problem directly and explicitly, thus shifting from epiphenomenal to deliberate problem solving in that area.

Such a shift presumably cannot take place for all problems. Some questions may be too disturbing to handle in any way except epiphenomenally. Delicate questions of policy of life and death—for example, on the allocation of transplanted organs in medical practice—are difficult to

---

3. Epiphenomenal solutions include both understood or analyzed solutions and interactive solutions. For example, the "solution" to the problem of resource allocation through market purchases and sales is both an interactive solution and an epiphenomenal solution. It is epiphenomenal because buyers and sellers solve it as a by-product of solving their own personal problems of earning a living.

approach explicitly and directly. People may prefer to leave them to be settled as by-products of physicians' technical decisions on individual therapy. Disturbing questions also include highly divisive issues like income distribution, which may be safer to alter as a by-product of specific policies for the aged, infirm, or needy.

Aside from Patrick Moynihan's proposal for "benign neglect" of certain racial problems, few pPSI have systematically asked which problems under what circumstances are (or should be) explicitly attacked and which problems are (or should be) resolved as by-products or epiphenomena. It is possible, of course, that answers cannot be had. But if the question were raised more often it would suggest a more restrained and appropriate sense of PSI's capacity on the part of pPSI.

PSI AND INTERACTIVE PROBLEM SOLVING

One set of misdirections and possible redirections of PSI needs considerable further specification at this point, so complex are they. They are those that arise in the relation of PSI to interactive problem solving as we have outlined it.

While it is possible to think of PSI (or any other analytical method) simply as an alternative to interactive problem solving, we have already seen that, when problem solving is interactive, there remains an altered and reduced role for PSI or other forms of analysis. Thus, when pPSI slight interactive problem solving, they frequently fail, we now suggest, to adapt problem solving to its altered and reduced role. A more careful tailoring of PSI to interaction would improve its effectiveness in social problem solving.

Consider a simple example. Hypothetically, the decision on a town's budget could be made directly and fully an analytic task. It could be approached as a research project. It rarely is, however. A more common possibility is that it is decided through voting, an interactive process. But voting does not, of course, wholly remove the need for analysis. Voters want some level of understanding before casting their votes. They may even wish to draw on PSI. Or PSI may be offered at the initiative of some participant —or more likely, some group. But the kind of analysis wanted or offered is not the same as would be required in the absence of voting had the decision on the budget been made directly and wholly a research task. Each voter may, for example, want only to understand "What's in it for me?" Or he may want to analyze only one or two issues that he intends to let govern his vote. His requirement for analysis, including PSI, will almost always be much less than the requirements of a research team aiming to produce a town budget.

Another example of adapting analysis (hence PSI) to interactive problem solving is in business problem solving. In market interactions, no one has to understand directly and solve the problem of resource allocation, as would be called for in a nonmarket economy. But all participants in market interaction, especially businessmen, instead face problems of whether to buy (or sell), what to buy, and how much to buy. For solving these simpler problems, analysis is still necessary, and businessmen invest heavily in certain forms of PSI in order to improve their decisions on these questions. But their use of PSI is obviously adapted to (as well as simplified by) their roles in market interactions. They seek to understand only what they need to know to play their interactive roles.

In contrast, many government officials are uncertain about their goals and responsibilities in social interaction, even if they are clear on the boundaries of their substantive assignment. As a result, some will pursue a broad public interest, others a narrower set of goals for which they believe they have been given special responsibility, and others will vacillate or remain ambiguous. Many officials in each of these three categories will thus fail to call on

PSI, as business executives do, to produce analysis specifically adapted to their particular problem-solving roles. Instead they may call for the impossible, as in the case of the Kerner Commission Report, which sought to deal with the problem of "white racism." Or such officials may maintain gloomily that PSI is of no help, not realizing that it can only rarely be of help with problems so globally defined.

At least two avenues of adaptation of PSI to interactive problem solving are always open. One is PSI that is helpful to participants in interaction because it provides information and analysis suited to their interactive roles. The other is PSI that diagnoses, evaluates, and improves the very process of social interaction. PSI intelligence on the Soviet Union made available to the State Department is an example of the former. PSI on reform of congressional rules is an example of the latter. PSI for a businessman is the former; PSI for an agency about to write new laws on fair-trade practices is the latter.

When PSI is provided only to help participants in an interactive process to play their parts, it is easy to distinguish it from PSI that makes a frontal attack on a problem on the supposition that it is to be solved wholly analytically and not interactively. But analysis directed to the evaluation, design, or restructuring of the interactive process itself can easily be confused with a frontal attack on the problem being handled in the interactive process. Beginning with dissatisfaction, say, with the distribution of income in the U.S.A., a pPSI might begin an analysis explicitly directed to the question (as though intending to push for an analytical solution to it): "In what pattern should income be distributed?" Or he might, from the outset or at any subsequent stage, turn instead to the questions: "Are market and/or political interactions of such a character as to achieve a desirable pattern of distribution?" The two questions are different, and the second does not necessarily require an answer to the first. On both points, confusion is easy to fall into.

Although professional economists do not explicitly formulate the issue of how PSI should be adapted to social interaction, their work habits show that they understand the necessity of the adaptation. Their characteristic specialty is analysis of market interaction. In their PSI they rarely ask about or express opinions about patterns of resource allocation. They do not trouble themselves to ask directly whether more of the nation's resources should go into food production, transportation, or any other line of production. Knowing that these questions are for the most part settled by market interactions, they ask questions about the market instead. Is this or that market structure sufficiently competitive to attain what would be presumed to be good resource allocation? Is this or that industry responding fully enough to market signals? The relative strength of economics as a discipline may be a consequence of working habits that reduce research to questions about interactions that solve economic problems rather than to questions that address the problems directly.

Other social scientific disciplines may show a much less sophisticated appreciation of social interaction as a method of social problem solving. Or it may be that the interactions relevant to their work are less visible, more difficult to perceive and understand, or less useful than market interactions as methods of social problem solving. For any of these reasons, the interactions might make it more difficult to adapt PSI to them. Whatever the reason, the consequence is that pPSI consequently seek what seem to be frontal attacks on problems rather than routinely adapt their research to problem-solving interaction. Perhaps trying to do too much, they achieve too little.

Practitioners of PSI who study city planning, for example, sometimes take as their problem the use of space for an entire city or neighborhood. Their work seems to deny the fact that certain interactive processes will inevitably solve many problems concerning the configuration of the city. They might therefore be well advised to study those interactions, simultaneously limiting their presumptions to those that can adapt to or restructure the existing interactions. Similarly, some students of public administration often take it upon themselves to design administrative systems in toto as though not realizing that every administrative organization works as it does because of characteristic interactive processes on which redesign must be built.

Strictly speaking, we suggest, all analysis is in fact teamed with some interactive problem solving. But pPSI differ greatly in the degree to which they understand that fundamental fact and tailor their work accordingly.

Partisan Use of PSI

If PSI is to be adapted to problem-solving interaction, it will sometimes be fashioned, we have just seen, to help a businessman learn how to earn a dollar, or a voter how to make the most of his small electoral voice, or a government official how to carry his program over the objection of his adversaries, or an interest-group leader how to win the most for his constituents. Even if the PSI is itself as objective or disinterested as possible, these *uses* of it are partisan in that they serve to advance the interests of persons who, playing roles in an interactive process, are necessarily partisan. With perhaps some rare and only imaginable exceptions, all participants in social interaction are partisans, even if not necessarily highly aggressive, irresponsible, narrow-minded, or bigoted. To adapt PSI to interactive problem solving—and our hypothesis is that it has to be so adapted to be effective—is thus to run contrary to a widespread belief that PSI should serve nonpartisan purposes.

Moreover, although many policy analysts understand and accept the commonplace partisan use of their studies, they believe that they themselves speak somehow for "the public interest" and do not understand the inevitably partisan character of their own work. Some policy analysts have claimed that pPSI are "partisans for the public interest"; but even that claim, which acknowledges a kind of partisanship, does not confess the partisanship embodied in their very *conception* of the public interest, which can no more wholly escape partisanship than can anyone else's. An economist, for example, dares to characterize the professional program evaluator as "the purveyor of the truth" in contrast to the policy maker, who is not.[4]

In any case, social scientists further removed from policy makers than are policy analysts tend toward the flat belief that their research should and can aspire to serve nonpartisan ends.[5] Perhaps the dominant ethic in research is a kind of neutrality. The conflict between their views and ours raises issues both as to fact and as to ethics.

As to issues of fact, perhaps the dominant belief is that the results of PSI move best into social problem solving when users are not committed to partisan positions but are instead, like the pPSI themselves, in some important senses neutral or uncommitted. Even if, as we have just suggested, all policy makers and problem solvers are partisan, we can distinguish between less and more partisanship and consider the possibility that the less the partisanship, the greater the likelihood that PSI can be fed into policy making and other forms of social problem solving.

A major problem is posed by the possibility that the facts are otherwise. It is partisans who appear to display an eagerness for the ammunition that new PSI findings pro-

4. John E. Brandl, "Evaluation and Politics," *Evaluation* (Special Issue, 1978), p. 6.
5. On an even stricter withdrawal from engagements in which scientific objectivity may lend strength to partisans, see, for example, Yaron Ezrahi, "The Jenson Controversy," in Charles Frankel, ed., *Controversies and Decisions* (New York: Russell Sage Foundation, 1976).

vide. To be sure, they may use the new findings corruptly. But when for partisan purposes they inject the new findings into public debate, their own PSI slips from their control and begins to play a role (as it is offered and challenged), often deeply effective, that it cannot play when no one cares greatly about it.

PSI would perhaps appropriately aspire to serve a non-partisan user if policy were made by a hypothetical policy maker pursuing the "public interest." But policy is actually made not by a policy maker but by interaction among a plurality of partisans. Each participant in the interaction, as noted above, needs information specialized to his partisan role in it.

Partisans, of course, come in different shapes and sizes. Some extremists discredit themselves; in their hands PSI often loses effect. At the opposite extreme, some people are partisans only in the sense that they pursue their own (hence partisan) version of the public interest. In that sense, members of the League of Women Voters are partisans. In between these extremes are a great variety of partisan pursuers of various segmental objectives: businessmen and their congressional allies, for example, looking for tax concessions; farmers and their Department of Agriculture allies looking for crop price supports. Our hypothesis is that through most of these partisans PSI is made an effective counter in policy negotiations. Relevant concepts, ideas, questions, and findings from PSI will be interjected into the debate because at least one partisan will find it to his advantage to do so. And conversely, the PSI may be challenged and scrutinized because at least one other partisan will find it to his advantage to do so.

That hypothesis obviously refers to a situation in which discussion is relatively open and proceeds with some respect for evidence. It may be, for example, that on issues in which moral choices are close to the surface (crime, abortion) partisanship works differently than it does in situations in which moral choices are more deeply buried (tax policy, science policy). But that is only one arbitrarily chosen example of possible variation.

If one finds, as we expect, that partisan channels are often the most efficient, then some common canons for some forms of PSI—those guiding academic social science, for example—will have to be amended, among them those that govern relations between pPSI and desired audience. It would not follow that a pPSI should bias his results to suit an audience, but it would seem to follow that in performing any given research he could usefully work for one of a variety of possible audiences and take his orientation not from an implicitly postulated "the" public interest, as is common, but from one of various explicitly recognized partisan interests each playing its role in the resolution of policy conflict. Many of the partisans will, of course, present their positions as versions of the public interest.

A Further Partisan Use of PSI: Weapons in a Damped Political Struggle

In social problem solving, partisans ordinarily find it too costly to fight to the death over their differences. Hence, they develop rules and procedures, explicit or tacit, that damp the conflict. These procedures range from the formality of voting, to the subtleties of reciprocal obligations: "You let me win this time, and I'll owe you one."

It appears that, in certain circumstances common especially in the bureaucracy, a tacit agreement comes into play according to which the victory goes to the superficial "winner" of the debate. We do not mean that those who concede are persuaded by the debate. But they in effect follow a tacit rule that declares that better evidence (especially better numbers) carries the day. As a result, PSI becomes a principal weapons maker in the struggle.

Such a practice makes further costly investment of effort

in a continuing struggle unnecessary, settles the issue peaceably, and does so by means of a ceremony that makes decision making appear to be informed and thoughtful, as indeed it is to a degree. Evidence and argument can in fact be fragmentary, provided only that by conventional superficial standards they are judged better than contrary evidence and argument.

We have participated in a number of interagency resolutions of their policy differences by what appeared to be just the mechanism described. We believe we have seen it operative in other areas too: university policy making, for example.

When it occurs, this kind of stylized partisan argument in policy making takes on some of the characteristics of the legal process. It has been noted that:

> When the correctness of a decision can be established unambiguously [as is not the case in PSI], the manner in which it is reached is largely immaterial; only results count. But when the factual and value premises are uncertain and controversial, when objective criteria of success or failure are lacking [as in PSI], the formal characteristics of the decision process—its procedure —becomes significant.[6]

The same point has been made with specific reference to PSI in the form of systems analysis or policy analysis.

> policy or systems analysis perform a function with respect to political-technological decisions similar to that performed by a judicial process. . . . A court decision is accepted by the disputing parties largely because it is based on a set of rules which both parties are prepared, before knowing its outcome, to accept as unbiased.[7]

6. Giandomenico Majone and Edward S. Quade, "Making Policy Analysis Safe," (unpublished mimeo, undated, but probably 1977).
7. Harvey Brooks, "Environmental Decision Making: Analysis and

Matched and Mismatched Cognitive Tactics:
Problem Solver and pPSI

If PSI is to be adapted to the needs of problem solvers engaged in social interaction rather than from Olympian heights detached from their needs, then it seems likely that the match between decision-reaching styles of pPSI and problem solver needs investigation.[8]

Although scholars are only slowly moving toward a clarification of the tactics of policy makers and other problem solvers, it seems reasonably clear that both pPSI, on one hand, and policy makers and other practical problem solvers, on the other, do attack their problems with a variety of invented tactics and that the tactics differ both from situation to situation and from person to person. Problem solving through successive approximation is one such tactic. Others (though they are not always sharply distinguishable) are: crisis decision making, bottleneck breaking, attending to the squeaky wheel, various forms of sequencing other than successive approximation, satisficing, routinized decision making by rule, and many methods of formal planning.

Tactics chosen by pPSI and problem solvers depend on at least two sets of factors: those bearing on their own *capabilities*—specifically, their cognitive capacity to cope with complex problems—and those bearing on their *incentives* to do so. Either because of capability or incentive considerations, a person—whether pPSI or problem solver—will refuse to attack some problems, or some form of problem, and attack others instead. At one extreme, a highly motivated, exceptionally confident person will try

Values," in L. H. Tribe, T. S. Schelling, and J. Voss, eds., *When Values Conflict* (Cambridge, Mass.: Ballinger, 1976), as quoted in Majone and Quade, "Making Policy Analysis Safe."

8. Earlier we defined a problem solver as a policy maker or other person (not a pPSI) who plays a practical role in social problem solving other than the PSI role. See above, p. 4.

for a comprehensive solution, once and for all, to a problem. At the other extreme, a less confident or less motivated one will bite off no more than a piece of his problem, leaving the other pieces for later bites, or bites by someone else. Since most big social problems in fact remain on the agenda for year after year, tactics may become extremely complex as the result of attempts on the part of the pPSI and problem solver to cope with the ever-shifting definition of the continuing problem.[9]

Since choice of tactic differs from person to person, hence between pPSI and policy maker, discrepancies arise between their respective tactics. One is tempted to believe that problem solving is advanced if pPSI and problem solver do not diverge in their choice of tactics. We need to examine that dubious hypothesis. Even if it is true, often the elimination of discrepancy between the two may be impossible for certain critical dimensions of problem solving, given the opposing strengths of academic conventions and the untidy pressures brought to bear on policy makers and other practical problem solvers. A scholar's approach to contemporary energy problems is not much like a congressman's. That being so, are there second-best tactics for the pPSI? How does he or can he minimize misfit?

But perhaps the elimination of the discrepancy is not an appropriate goal even if it were possible. It may be that the discordant tactics which the pPSI brings to the service of the policy maker create a special illumination or stimulus. A bureaucrat who thinks small may need and want a pPSI advisor who thinks big.

9. Many students of problem-solving tactics have discussed capabilities as they bear on problem solving, Herbert Simon among others. Relatively few have grappled with fundamental aspects of incentives. One who has is Albert Hirschman, in *The Strategy of Economic Development* (New Haven: Yale University Press, 1958). See also Albert Hirschman and Charles E. Lindblom, "Economic Development, Research and Development, Policy Making: Some Converging Views," *Behavioral Science*, vol. 7 (April 1962).

We know very little about these issues of matching or mismatching problem-solving tactics of pPSI and problem solvers. Given the wide circulation of conventional notions about rational problem solving, pPSI have not looked deeply into the differing tactics that intellectual and practical problem solvers use.

Problems in achieving a productive adaptation of pPSI tactics to problem solvers' tactics do not arise solely when a pPSI/client relationship exists. Even if the pPSI studies his problem in academe with no particular client in mind, his choice of tactics may either facilitate or obstruct his communication with readers who can or cannot respond to his tactics. Readers may either dismiss or admire a pPSI as, say, utopian because his method of analysis does not take the many "practical" turns their own minds take.

The Power of pPSI in Democratic Government

A final set of questions on the relation between analysis and interaction as alternative methods of social problem solving turns on a certain hostility between PSI and political democracy. Many pPSI, we have suggested, are insensitive or actually hostile to a large role for social interaction in social problem solving. Their espousal of PSI is often explicitly stated in the form of a condemnation of "politics"—even democratic politics. Or a hostility to democracy appears in the ethic of nonpartisan neutrality and in associated ideas about the role of scientific expertise in the decision process. For example, although much of the resistance among pPSI to private client-oriented work is said to be justified as a way to preserve neutrality, the source of the resistance may in fact be an attachment to the greater power associated with the role of independent expert. Perhaps then pPSI have perceptions and attitudes concerning their own power that are inconsistent with certain aspects of political democracy.

One of the paradoxes of political democracy in the nation state, still not yet widely appreciated, is that its ordinary citizens have good reason to feel almost as impotent as the citizens of an authoritarian regime. For insofar as genuine democracy is approximated, power is equally distributed among millions of citizens, with the consequence that no single citizen enjoys more than a tiny, nearly useless share. So widely are power, authority, and influence distributed in large democratic systems like that of the U.S.A. that even presidents and prime ministers, congressmen, senators, and M.P.'s often despair of mobilizing enough support to carry through their preferred policies. As President Truman said of the president's authority, "He'll say, 'Do this! Do that!' And nothing will happen."[10]

It may be that pPSI similarly suffer from some of the same feelings of impotence. If at some points democracy historically has been interpreted to be a device to bring reason to bear on policy, it is at other points a device to frustrate it—to make sure that no small group, not even one that may think it knows what needs to be done, can achieve a greatly disproportionate influence on policy. Practitioners of PSI may also not understand that democracy poses additional special obstacles to PSI in social problem solving, among which is the necessity, on some policy issues, for an extremely broad diffusion of new knowledge, a requirement to which most pPSI seem indifferent, indeed often disdaining those who attempt such a diffusion.

Since knowledge is power, part of the price that society must pay for increasing use of PSI is to let power to some degree slide into the hands of pPSI. Just how does it in fact slide? And to what extent can the slide be controlled? For what kinds of authority or other power—in what conditions and on what kind of issues—is it most important that the

---

10. Richard E. Neustadt, *Presidential Power* (New York: John Wiley & Sons, 1960), p. 9.

slide be resisted? Is ineffective PSI a requisite of political democracy? What might be the effects on democracy of a substantially more effective PSI? How do problems of effective PSI relate to problems posed by meritocracy? The questions are no less important for being familiar.

6. Alternatives to Authoritativeness

The reduction of PSI to a competitive and complementary relation to other inputs into social problem solving is attributable not exclusively but most fundamentally, we have suggested, to the complexity of the social world that PSI seeks to understand. In some large part, PSI is reduced to that relation because it fails, in the face of that complexity, to achieve a quality we have called independent authoritativeness. We have further suggested that usually PSI is misdirected when it pursues a kind of authoritativeness that it cannot ordinarily achieve.

One alternative to the pursuit of independent authoritativeness is the pursuit of dependent authoritativeness. In chapter 4 we indicated why that alternative is and must often be taken—why PSI must therefore be pursued in intricate relation with ordinary knowledge, without which PSI is not sufficiently conclusive and therefore not authoritative. The other alternative is to pursue objectives other than authoritativeness—thus pursuing neither independent nor dependent authoritativeness. We shall now examine that alternative.

For some pPSI, it is difficult to imagine any other objective for PSI than the achievement of authoritativeness, or at least of an approximation to scientific conclusiveness, which is the principal component of authoritativeness. As we noted, the very idea of scientific inquiry seems to imply conclusiveness and, through it, authoritativeness. Yet there are alternatives for PSI; it does not have to be authoritative to be useful. Redirection of its efforts is called for, however, if it is to pursue alternatives when authoritativeness is only a will-o'-the-wisp.

One might suppose that the functions of PSI for social problem solving would be well codified in the literature of social science; but the process has only begun.[1]

ENLIGHTENMENT VERSUS ENGINEERING

In some minds, only social engineers need authoritative knowledge—that is to say, only pPSI who are pushing for specific practicable solutions to well-defined problems. A common formulation of a major alternative and non-authoritative role for PSI is as "enlightenment."[2] When one casts about for examples of PSI's contribution to social problem solving, the most obvious examples are not the social engineering studies offered to government agencies, but seem to be the more fundamental enlightenment of thought achieved by such pPSI as Adam Smith, Marx, Freud, and Dewey.

Some will object to an enlightenment-engineering comparison that rests on the accomplishments of the great figures in intellectual history. They will say that what one occasional great mind can achieve throws little light on alternative possibilities open to pPSI generally. The objection raises an interesting issue. Now that PSI is an ubiquitous feature of contemporary life, at least in the wealthier parts of the world, is it possible that it can steadily

1. A number of relatively recent studies are beginning to sort out PSI functions. For example, Martin Greenberger, Matthew A. Crenson, and Brian L. Crissey, *Models in the Policy Process* (New York: Russell Sage Foundation, 1967), pp. 329 and 332–36. See also, Carol H. Weiss, ed., *Using Social Research in Public Policy Making*.

2. For one of many examples, engineering and enlightenment are compared in M. Janowitz, *Political Conflict* (Chicago: University of Chicago Press, 1970), pp. 305–21. For development of this theme, see David K. Cohen and Michael S. Garet, "Reforming Educational Policy with Applied Social Research," *Harvard Educational Review* 45 (February 1975).

achieve—through a collectivity of pPSI rather than through a rare seminal mind—the same kind of pervasive enlightenment that we attribute to the seminal mind?[3] Is, for example, the input-output analytical approach to social process that is now practiced in a number of the social sciences a major contribution to social theory comparable to those we owe to those seminal minds? If not widely recognized, is that approach undervalued only because it gradually emerged from the scholarly community without attribution to any particular originator?

Although some such distinction as engineering versus enlightenment is an old one, a precise formulation of the alternatives has not yet been achieved. Nevertheless, the idea of enlightenment rather than social engineering at least opens up for consideration a wide-ranging set of intellectual tasks for PSI in which the conclusiveness and authoritativeness of propositions may be of less importance than other aspects of the task that need further study before they are well sorted out and understood. It may be that, without achieving conclusiveness or authoritativeness—or for that matter without developing testable scientific propositions—PSI is nevertheless capable of clarifying man's understanding of the social world.

The idea of progress, an idea of enormous consequence to man in approaching social problems, is not quite a proposition; nor could it ever be conclusively established. The same can be said for Marx's economic determinism, or structural functionalism, or the purposive, rational, calculating man who increasingly stalks the pages of theoretical social science. Not being propositions, they cannot be tested; and not being tested, they cannot be conclusive.

3. One might ponder—and doubt—that possibility by examining a list of alleged social science breakthroughs in Karl W. Deutsch, John Platt, and Dieter Senghas, "Conditions Favoring Major Advances in Social Science," *Science*, vol. 171 (February 5, 1971).

Thus they cannot be authoritative in any sense, though they can be decisive. But these ideas suggest a role for PSI, even if not yet well understood, that does not turn on its authoritativeness.

Some natural scientists find an engineering-enlightenment distinction incorrect in reference to the functions of natural science. In their eyes, engineering knowledge is not science. In fact, engineering knowledge, they find, arises and still remains surprisingly independent of science. If the study of the social world is on these points parallel to their view of the physical world, then "enlightenment" and "engineering" may refer to intellectual activities much further apart than pPSI appear to believe. Good social engineering may require a more autonomous intellectual tradition than has been granted it in PSI, and one greatly removed from social science. And perhaps, unlike the physical sciences, the social sciences might be developed as nonauthoritative, while social engineering pursues authoritativeness.

It is, however, still a commonplace in much of the literature that social science develops and confirms (at least probabilistically) broad, enlightening exploratory generalizations which through applied social research (thus engineering) are then applied to solutions to actual social problems. Such a view challenges the suggestion just made that the pursuit of enlightenment may excuse PSI from a pursuit of authoritativeness. But two objections have been registered to this conventional interpretation. The first is that with relatively few exceptions (largely in psychology and economics), social science does not in fact produce and confirm generalizations.[4] Those that are produced are greatly lacking in conclusiveness and authoritativeness.

The second is that "applied" researchers or "social en-

4. Ernest Nagel, *The Structure of Science* (New York: Harcourt, Brace, and World, 1961), p. 447.

gineers" do not in fact often apply such generalizations as
are produced by social scientists. Instead, what is ordinarily called "applied research" is an effort of distinctive
character in its own right, developing its own generalizations, when needed, through its own efforts.[5] In short,
when social engineers need authoritative knowledge, they
must develop it for themselves.

Some science historians, moreover, find it necessary to
distinguish in natural science between "engineering" in
the ordinary sense and another kind of intellectual inquiry
that is neither quite engineering nor science. It is the exploration of new technological possibilities opened up by
scientific advances—for example, space exploration or,
perhaps, cloning.[6] It is open-ended exploratory activity
that uses but does not necessarily create new scientific
knowledge. Nor does it settle into the design of new
technologies, as does engineering.

If social science is in this respect like natural science,
there are important functions to be performed falling between enlightenment and engineering. These may be
unique kinds of inquiry into, speculation about, and design
of the social world that differ from the analysis of particular policies or policy problems. They require the exploration of "social space." Barrington Moore, Jr., for one,
argues that social science can best show "the range of
possible alternatives and the potentiality for effective action."[7] In these possibilities, there appear to be opportunities for a nonauthoritative PSI.

5. Alvin W. Gouldner, "Explorations in Applied Social Science," in
Gouldner and S. M. Miller, eds., *Applied Sociology* (New York: Free
Press, 1975), pp. 6–7.
6. See James R. Killian, Jr., "Capsule Conclusions," in Dael Wolfle,
ed., *Symposium on Basic Research* (Washington: American Association
for the Advancement of Science, 1959), pp. 122–23; and Edward Teller,
"The Role of Applied Science," in National Academy of Sciences, *Basic
Research and National Goals* (Washington, 1965), p. 260.
7. Barrington Moore, Jr., *Political Power and Social Theory* (New
York: Harper, 1962), p. 159.

Conceptualization

Some attempts have been made to specify just what enlightenment and its cousins consist of. PSI enlightens, some people say, not through new information or even through sustained analysis, but through the new conceptualization that it either provides or stimulates. In one formulation:

> Social research can be "used" in reconceptualizing the character of policy issues or even redefining the policy agenda. Thus, social research may sensitize decision makers to new issues and turn what were nonproblems into policy problems (a current controversial example is "white flight"). In turn, it may convert existing social problems into nonproblems (e.g., marijuana use). It may drastically revise the way that a society thinks about issues, (e.g., acceptable rates of unemployment), the facets of an issue that are viewed as susceptible to alteration, and the alternative measures that it considers.[8]

These would all appear to be alternatives to the pursuit of authoritative knowledge, even if they are also helpful to such a pursuit.

PSI influence on intellectual frameworks of policy makers. With reference to conceptualization, a particular noteworthy phenomenon is a convergence among policy makers similar to convergence among scientists on analytical frameworks, such as, for example, those Thomas Kuhn calls paradigms. That is to say, policy makers attack specific problems in the light of a general framework or perspective that controls both explanatory hypotheses and range of solutions that they are willing to consider. In his study of policy on juvenile delinquency, for example,

---

8. Carol H. Weiss, Introduction, in Weiss, ed., *Using Social Research in Public Policy Making*, pp. 15–16.

Alfred J. Kahn has shown the dominance among policy makers of such a framework.[9]

Although the connection between framework or paradigm in social science and what we are here calling a policy-making framework appears to be extremely loose, a connection indeed appears to exist. The policy-making framework is derived from PSI. In Kahn's study, it appears that his policy makers at first shared a framework of thought that represented their loose understanding of academic psychology. They subsequently abandoned it, only to take up in its place another that represented their equally loose understanding of academic sociology.[10] Again it appears that PSI offers a contribution that does not take the form of authoritative knowledge.

Of course, one might argue from such a case as Kahn's that academic social science is no more than window dressing for policy strategies chosen on other grounds. Or that it only marginally strengthens or refines policy-making frameworks chosen on practical grounds. Nor need we deny the dependence of pPSI on historically earlier frameworks which they take from elsewhere in society— from practical problem solvers, for example, or from ordinary knowledge on which PSI is, in this respect as in others earlier identified, dependent. All these possibilities aside, in the immediate situation the dependence of problem solvers on PSI frameworks may be close; and the frameworks provided by PSI may be sturdy and lasting.

Hence, even if policy makers do not turn to PSI in many

9. Alfred J. Kahn, "From Delinquency Treatment to Community Development" in Lazarsfeld, Sewell, and Wilensky, eds., *The Uses of Sociology* pp. 477–505.

10. In Kahn's example, however, it cannot be said that the policy-making paradigm *followed* some movement in social science, only that the shift had origins in competing doctrines in social science. Moreover, Kahn observes that the shift could not be said to be a product of research that justified it nor that social scientists made any case for it. Policy makers simply chose it.

of the ordinarily expected ways—for specific data, hypotheses, evidence, or policy evaluation—they may take the whole organizing framework or perspective for their work from academic social science. It may be decisive though not authoritative. It is possible that this is sometimes the major contribution of PSI to social problem solving.

Indirections and Lags

One implication of much of the above is that PSI may, as a condition of making some of its most significant contributions to social problem solving, be required to accept substantial lags and indirections in achieving an influence.

An obvious example here is Keynesian economics. It achieved its full effects in the U.S.A. only after a generation's delay, becoming dominant in American policy making with a lag from the 1930s to the 1960s. And it may have achieved its effect largely by complex indirection. Keynesian theory first moved from professional economists to graduate students. Then, as the latter moved into faculty positions, wrote textbooks, and taught undergraduates, they planted a rough understanding of Keynesian thought that was thereafter carried into legislatures and bureaucracies when their students left the classroom and eventually moved into positions of influence in policy making.

The study of a number of such lagged and complicated transmissions is potentially all the more informative because transmission moves at different rates in different countries—in the Keynesian case much faster in some countries than in the U.S.A.

Another phenomenon of lags can also be illustrated from economics. Economists made monetary and fiscal economics—macrotheory—their principal concern only after the nation had begun to climb out of the Depression, thus at least ten or fifteen years too late to help decisions about how to avoid the Depression. Similarly, economists turned much of their attention to international trade only after World War II, when restoration of trade abruptly became urgent. But again they were too late, because urgent practical problems could not wait for ten years or more for their refinement of international trade theory. Economists were again caught unprepared by the practical problems of developing the Third World to which the industrialized nations then turned. Again they flocked into a field of research for which answers were already too late, at least in the sense that decisions to undertake development had already been taken.

Does such a record imply a need for PSI to understand and thus overcome lagged and complex transmission? Or do they suggest that slow and indirect paths are an acceptable route for PSI ideas?

Conversion of PSI into ordinary knowledge. When lags are very long, some PSI knowledge passes into general circulation either among elites or in the population as a whole. A great deal of economic knowledge, for example, from Smith, Ricardo, the Austrians, Marshall, and Keynes is now detached from its sources. It has been taken up by persons who have accepted it, despite their ignorance of the evidence or argument on which it rests. They have taken it in much the same way they take, earlier in their lives, information that the earth is round. Much of this economic information is not conclusive. They take it as a basis for action despite its scientific inconclusiveness. Yet much of it, most economists would say, is more probably true than the knowledge it displaced or amended.

Is this the way that PSI makes its principal contribution to social problem solving? Many pPSI may consider this to be a demeaning suggestion, but it is not. It leaves enormous scope for PSI and leaves open the possibility that PSI is of pivotal consequence for the world in ways removed from the conventional pursuit of scientific conclusiveness and authoritativeness. It does, however, point to a no less great change of direction for study and research. The question is well worth exploring, even if the exploration itself will be inconclusive.

EVIDENCE AND ARGUMENT

PSI can perform functions easily confused with the achievement of authoritativeness. They are best perceived if seen embedded in the give-and-take of policy making.

Fact and Proof versus Evidence and Argument

Despite the accepted convention that pPSI are engaged in the pursuit of conclusive fact and proof, they are instead engaged in producing inconclusive evidence and argument. Problem complexity denies the possibility of proof and reduces the pursuit of fact to the pursuit of those selective facts which, if appropriately developed, constitute evidence in support of relevant argument. We do not mean here that evidence is manufactured without respect to data, or that contrary evidence is suppressed, or that argument is indifferent to such facts as can be established. We mean only to call attention to the inevitably incomplete character of attempts at proof, the consequent reduction of such attempts to informed argument, and the highly selective search for just those facts that bear on argument as evidence for or against the argued position. There is, consequently, a need for new rules of verification or proof suitable to what PSI can actually accomplish.

Majone has made these points with reference to policy analysis.[11] We suggest that his insight can be generalized to almost all forms of PSI, including much of its social scientific component as well.

11. Giandomenico Majone, "The Uses of Policy Analysis," in Russell Sage Foundation, *Annual Report*, 1977–78, p. 202 and passim.

Post-Decision PSI

Judges write their opinions after they make their judicial decisions. The opinion serves to commend the decision to others. Writing it may also clarify the judge's mind on the relation of the decision to other decisions he had made, thus organizing his mind in ways helpful to his coping with future decisions. The relation of issues in the judicial opinion to those issues that actually brought him to his decision may either be close or distant.

Majone goes on to suggest that by a very rough parallel, a good deal of PSI is contracted for or otherwise produced in order to display the rationality of decisions reached through ordinary knowledge. But, he adds, PSI is not simply a rationalization of decisions already reached—in the pejorative sense of the term *rationalization*. It may test the decision, that is, ask whether grounds can be found through PSI for setting aside a decision reached through ordinary knowledge and analysis. It also may commend the decision to others without whose consent it cannot be made effective. It also satisfies strong desires of decision makers to see their decisions in a perspective of rational thought, and that is in many cases a useful form of self-testing.[12]

In all these post-decision uses of PSI, it is not authoritative for action, coming as it does after the act. Some pPSI will allege that these are misuses of PSI. Clearly, however, much of PSI is of this character; and it is important to clarify, by further research, the possibility that much or most of PSI is destined, in ways that cannot be escaped, for unauthoritative uses of these kinds. The closer PSI moves to direct engagement in social problem solving—as, for example, when the pPSI takes a policy-making organization as client—the more difficult it is to find examples of PSI that are in their impact unquestionably pre- rather than

12. Ibid.

post-decision, hence authoritative for the decision.

It is just possible, at an extreme, that PSI infrequently achieves authoritativeness for action through putting previous decisions in intellectual order by post-decision defense of them, thus indirectly altering the perspective through which subsequent decisions are made. Think of Adam Smith's *Wealth of Nations* in this light.

REPORTING

In recounting what PSI has and has not achieved in policy making in Washington, Rivlin calls our attention to the now vastly improved knowledge held by policy makers of just what their problems are. We now know as never before just who the poor are, where they are, and what it is they lack. More than ever before, we know which parts of the nation are growing and which are not; which parts of our cities are less or more troubled by street crime or urban decay; who among the nation's children are or are not learning to read.[13]

Without deprecating this great accomplishment, we take note that it looks more like reporting than science. Yet if pPSI aspire to authoritativeness, it is in this modest activity that they will most frequently succeed. Compared to the task of achieving scientific generalization, it is easy work and surer of result. And its successes, especially when set beside the continuing inability of academic social scientists to develop more than a few scattered authoritative scientific generalizations, suggest that it may represent a contribution by PSI to social problem solving more significant than what they have achieved or can ever achieve through the pursuit of authoritative scientific generalization.

The possibility raises questions to be explored. If we consider a continuum with nomothetic generalization at

---

13. Alice M. Rivlin, *Systematic Thinking for Social Action*, (Washington, D.C.: Brookings Institution, 1971).

one extreme and simple reporting (say, on the incomes of Puerto Rican families in New York City) at the other, we can ask where various kinds of PSI are located on the continuum. We also can ask whether some locations appear to be more helpful to social problem solving than others. In general, we would be looking at PSI without the blinders ordinarily imposed by reverence for authoritativeness at the level of scientific generalization and by disdain for the reporting services formerly reserved only for journalists.

PSI AS ART OR RITUAL

Finally, it is always a popular sport in some circles to deny that even such great figures in the history of thought as Adam Smith, Marx, and Freud achieved any effect other than articulating with skill a body of understanding already broadly current in society. If this was their role, it is not to be deprecated. Such a role is a useful one, even if conventional accounts of how social science operates would miss it. Perhaps such a figure is more artist than scientist. If so, he presumably plays a role in social problem solving different from what is usually attributed to him. The possibility is not frivolous and bears examination as another alternative to authoritativeness.

Taking a different view of PSI, it can be asked whether it is practiced for the same reason as, say, dancing in tribal societies. It is on many points interesting to watch, even more interesting to participate in. Its rituals are designed to bring assurance; and no doubt even otherwise futile PSI often does so, simply because some people feel better if they make their decisions after the ceremonies of analysis, no matter how inconclusive the analysis. It also brings assurance because it appears to apply the prestigious effective methods of natural science to the study of the social world. As a ritual, PSI might serve still other functions worth searching for.

Beyond the suggestions of this chapter, it seems clear that the literature of PSI should be culled over to look for contributions to social problem solving obscured by the common preoccupation with authoritative knowledge.

For each of the functions that PSI performs as an alternative to its pursuit of authoritative propositions, new guidelines or understanding need to be explored for pPSI. We suggest that, currently, many pPSI are preoccupied with authoritativeness and habitually undervalue PSI's other services to social problem solving. They therefore remain silent on PSI practices suitable to these other services; or, what is worse, limit pPSI to performing fruitless exercises in pursuing the alternatives to authoritativeness while being bound by rules that fit only the pursuit of authoritativeness. The strain on PSI produces both distortion and comic effects, the latter in circumstances in which concepts and frameworks, none of which can be authoritative in any case, are debated as though they could be subjected to the same tests as verifiable propositions. Examples are many disputes on concepts like sovereignty, democracy, social function, and competition. A reconsideration of guidelines would liberate PSI to perform explicitly and with increasing skill problem-solving functions now frequently crippled or in clouded repute.

7. Compounding Error

A reader of an earlier draft of this manuscript put the question to us: "Do you want only to suggest that PSI fails to do as well as it might, or do you want also to suggest that it often positively obstructs social problem solving?" We want to suggest both. And we can do so by looking at some additional conspicuous features of PSI. Their effect is a PSI on some counts overblown, pretentious, and meddling—in these respects a positive obstruction to social problem solving. On other counts, the effect is PSI's inattention to important problems—in these respects deliquent.

WASTE

One feature is the relatively thoughtless wastefulness of PSI, which can be viewed simply as failure. But if inappropriate projects and practices waste PSI resources, the waste can also be viewed as obstructive. Examples are the proliferation of research on almost every topic that occurs to anyone and the expensive collection of rapidly obsolescent data (as has been argued to be the case for many voting studies).

For another example, government agencies are again and again assigned (by the legislature or by superior agencies) responsibilities beyond any person's or organization's known competence. They do not typically resist these assignments because they are funded and maintained for their efforts, not for their results. Hence, for example, appropriations to drug-abuse control agencies continue year after year, despite the absence of result.[1] The impossible tasks

1. Mark H. Moore, "Reorganization Plan #2 Reviewed: Problems in the Implementation of a Strategy to Reduce Supplies of Drugs to Illicit Markets in the U.S.," in Edith Stokey, ed., *Public Policy*, vol. 28 (New

set these overextended agencies then lead to wastefulness because of consequent impossible assignments of tasks to PSI.

Wasteful PSI, however, is perhaps more a result of poor project choices by pPSI themselves than of wasteful projects called for by users of PSI, since most pPSI select their own projects without reference to any particular client. Convinced, as we believe they often are, that PSI has problem-solving abilities far beyond what it actually does possess, pPSI have never attended seriously and professionally to project choice—or to the larger question of how so scarce and costly a resource as PSI should be deployed in society.

Confident of the utility of any and all PSI, its practitioners often choose problems or topics without much thought about—and no extended professional study of—the probable cost and usefulness of the results. The professionalism with which they execute given research projects sharply contrasts with the personal and subjective way in which they choose them: "I got started along this track in graduate school," or "It's what I enjoy doing," or "It's a topic that lends itself to the tools I know how to use."

Even the more thoughtful attempts to justify project choice—for example, those that appear in applications for research funds—are typically prefatory and tentative, more casual than seriously studied. In some preliminary studies, we have interrogated willing social scientists on their rationales for project choice. The justification of their projects appeals not to developed knowledge of how and when social science is or is not useful, but simply to judgments about the "importance" of the problem to be studied. Except on the assumption, which we are challenging, that PSI is always an appropriate cure for a problem, judgment

York: John Wiley & Sons, for the Kennedy School of Government, Harvard University, 1978).

about the importance of a problem is a naïve and wholly indefensible guide to research priorities.

Projects are often justified on the ground that all knowledge is valuable. Since sooner or later we need to know everything we can, any well-designed project is thought to be worth doing. It is a measure of amateurishness in project choice that those pPSI who so argue do not take the next step in their logic of project justification. For if the value of PSI is in fact so high as to promise returns on almost any kind of investigation, then PSI ought to be considered a resource so precious as not to be squandered. Its assumed high value does not justify a relatively indiscriminate endorsement of any project, but calls instead for careful allocation. Indeed, allocation of research resources is an important economic problem.[2]

NOISE IN THE SYSTEM

We have suggested that some problems call for interactive rather than analyzed solutions or for ordinary rather than PSI knowledge. But for many of these problems, pPSI go on writing and talking as though they were making a contribution to the solution. The effect is often to introduce distraction or noise into problem solving—a positive obstruction to social problem solving. The noise is now very loud and sometimes—PSI debate on race and schooling are good examples—almost deafening. It is almost impossible for pPSI to acknowledge the possibility that their very words are part of the problem rather than part of the solution.

To be sure, the noise is not—at least obviously—wholly attributable to pPSI inattention to their limited contribution

---

2. Certain parallels between research planning and economic planning are illuminating—as, for example, in the balanced growth controversy. See Albert O. Hirschman and Charles E. Lindblom, "Economic Development, Research and Development, Policy Making: Some Converging Views," *Behavioral Science*, vol. 7 (April 1962).

and their predisposition to offer their services even where not needed. Another cause of the noise is the new institutional position of PSI in society. Considering the number of pPSI now practicing, the growth in funds devoted to PSI in the years since World War II, its ubiquity in government, and its emerging new role in Western culture, it must now be regarded as one of society's major and noisiest institutions, comparable to political parties, the media, or business enterprises.

A particular feature of PSI—other than its growth rate and contemporary scale—to which pPSI seem so far to have given inadequate attention, is its new prominence in, and presumable impact on, popular culture. PSI is now rountinely in the news; and PSI books, even journal articles and technical reports from the Government Printing Office, and pronouncements of prominent pPSI are, as contemporary jargon describes them, "media events." *Psychology Today* thrives on the publication of PSI in psychology for ordinary readers. The Coleman reports produce widespread editorial comments, as well as continuing controversy in the press. Professors Milton Friedman and James Tobin debate fine points of stabilization policy for a television audience. In the original school desegregation case, the Supreme Court drew on sociological PSI and consequently placed the findings on the agenda of public debate. John Kenneth Galbraith, through books and a television series, wins no less firm a place as a public figure than do Senator Byrd, Robert McNamara, David Rockefeller, Tom Seaver, or Truman Capote.

The prominent institutionalization and popularization of PSI as a source of noise in the system may not be independent of the noise attributable to the disposition of pPSI to offer their services uncritically in all circumstances and to all possible users. But, to some degree, their own claims and ambitions explain the institutionalization and popularization of PSI.

"POLICY ANALYSIS" AND SYSTEMS ANALYSIS

It is also possible that certain now prestigious forms of PSI are frequently obstructive to social problem solving, despite their great usefulness in other applications. An increasingly prestigious view among pPSI on how they can best contribute to social problem solving explicitly turns the whole of problem solving over to PSI in a particular form. It is called "policy analysis."[3] A common variant is systems analysis.

In this approach, it is the obligation of the pPSI to go through all the steps necessary to a social problem's solution (which he can then recommend to a decision maker). The identification and definition of the problem, the canvassing of methods by which it might be ameliorated, the investigation of the implications of each of the various methods, the weighing of implications against each other, the final aggregation of all relevant considerations into a specific policy recommendation—all these become tasks for pPSI.[4]

In actual complex problem solving, however, most of all this activity—defining, estimating, weighing, and judging—is accomplished through practical judgment, a form of ordinary analysis. It is therefore not out of the question that PSI can often be much more useful by limiting itself to highly selective contributions to policy debate. Or alternatively—but this casts PSI in a role to which many academic social scientists would object—PSI could incorporate the professional practice of exerting practical judgment. The art of practical judgment could become, then, part of the training of all "social scientists" or all of the training of some "social scientists."

3. Although "policy analysis" has other meanings as well.

4. See, for an idealized form of such an approach, Herbert J. Gans, "Social Science for Public Policy," in Irving Louis Horowitz, ed., *The Use and Abuse of Social Science*, 2d ed. (New Brunswick, N.J.: Transaction Books, 1975).

Already, earlier enthusiasm for highly scientific "policy analysis" and systems analysis looks naïve, an indication that we have only begun to think carefully about the competing attractions of formal completeness of analysis, on the one hand, and selective contribution, on the other—and about the competing attractions of science and art in problem solving. We do not suggest that systems analysis is bankrupt, only that its place needs further investigation.

HYPER-RATIONALISM AMONG pPSI

Waste, noise, and the excesses of "policy analysis" all reflect, we suggest, a kind of hyper-rationalism among pPSI. As a result of inattention to the limited contribution of PSI to social problem solving so far, pPSI often succumb to the belief that, given enough PSI, all social problems can be significantly ameliorated by it. In actual historical fact, the "solution" to many social problems is simply continuing suffering. Or repression. Or a solution that itself creates new problems. That these bleak prospects can be greatly altered by PSI is a matter of faith not evidence. To believe, as a thoughtful person might, that societies can make significant headway against social problems does not imply that they can do so through PSI. For, as we have suggested, much of the world's work of problem solving is accomplished not through PSI but through ordinary knowledge, through social learning, and through interactive problem solving.

On many counts, therefore, social problem solving is—and will continue to be—a process removed from "rational problem solving." More than by the word *rational*, social problem solving, or aspects of it, should be characterized as unmanageable, fitful, erratic, and even by such words as *cruel* and *mindless*, though it cannot be both at once. A realistic view of social problem solving stands in contrast to the rationalistic view implicit among the most enthusiastic advocates of PSI.

If one were to look only at the last two decades, one might come away with an impression of linear growth in such rationalistic approaches. But if one begins at the turn of this century, the Progressive appetite for rationalistic reforms might make the development appear to be more cyclical, or perhaps wavelike.

A CONSEQUENT SUGGESTED PRESCRIPTION

Because these pages propose a research program rather than report on work already accomplished, specific implications for the improved practice of PSI for social problem solving remain largely to be discovered. We have only indicated their direction and illustrated some possibilities. At this point, however, we offer one further specific prescription, perhaps valuable itself but in any case indicative of work that needs to be done. When a pPSI contemplates research on any one of the countless projects over which PSI now ranges or might be extended to encompass, the most frequently applicable prescription for him is "Stop!" Even for important problems, questions, or issues, the most frequently appropriate course of action of a pPSI is to leave it alone.

Given the resources available for PSI, even if they were multiplied many times, and given such inescapable built-in limitations on its capacity as we have discussed, PSI can investigate only a small number of all the important issues open to investigation. A prerequisite to a more effective use of PSI is selectivity or discrimination—which implies substituting a general disposition to say no for the contemporary disposition of pPSI to say yes to almost any important problem now proposed or imagined for them.

An intelligent discrimination is not easy to achieve. None of us now engaged in PSI knows how to achieve it. It requires such studies as here proposed into the relation of PSI to ordinary knowledge, social learning, and interactive problem solving. Thus, it requires fundamental new insights into how certain kinds of specialized professional knowledge can best be laid over ordinary knowledge and how scholarly or professional research can best play a problem-solving role in tandem with interactive processes. Again, PSI does not simply operate against a background of political, economic, and social interaction. Instead it is intimately intertwined with interaction. Interactive problem solving, we have stressed, is both complementary and competitive with analytical problem solving. Hence, no pPSI can achieve a high degree of discrimination about what he studies without understanding the complexity of the complementary and competitive relations of PSI to the other inputs, and thoughtfully drawing implications from them for his own practice.

"Stop!" is an essential prescription. But of course the next, more thoughtful, and in the long run more helpful prescription is to reconsider the character of social problem solving through PSI. We do not, of course, recommend that practitioners of it sit on their hands. All these pages add up not to a rejection of PSI, despite the severity of some of our comments, but to a proposal that pPSI study, think about, and reconsider some of the most venerable of beliefs and practices about how PSI is made useful to social problem solving. And, of course, in particular we stress the need for meticulous attention to the need for a better understanding of the relation of PSI to other inputs into social problem solving, and of the need for other outputs because PSI cannot ordinarily be independently authoritative.

OTHER FAILURES AND OBSTRUCTIONS

Another family of failures and obstructions stems from familiar aspects of social science and PSI that we have, because of their familiarity, not hitherto developed in our analysis. Among them are issues concerning "arbitrary" factors in—often constraints on—problem formulation.

They are not in fact arbitrary—indeed, one would want to research their causes. They look arbitrary, however, and call PSI into question. For "no good reason," it appears, some obvious problems are simply ignored in PSI; or aspects of them are simply dropped. It looks as though a variety of influences, such as underlying metaphysical position, intellectual tradition, changing intellectual fashions, and moral or aesthetic prohibitions (much like the taboos that anthropologists find in all societies) are at work.

An example is the exclusion from academic economics of the problems of the underdeveloped countries until after World War II, when a whole new subfield developed around them. A similar switch in fashion in economics moved public-sector economics from the wasteland of professionally deprecated topics to a now prestigious position. A remarkable feature of American political science, shared to some extent with other social sciences, was its long-time implicit denial of the existence of a large population of blacks in our society. Formal treatises on democratic theory generalized about the American system with propositions not believable except on the assumption that the black population did not exist.

These "arbitrary" constraints are sometimes of broad scope. In the heyday of pluralist thought in American political science, almost every pluralist apparently knew that socioeconomic class accounted for grave inequalities in political influence and for important forms of elite dominance. Yet these were omitted from his more formal attempts at theory building or synoptic description of the political process.[5]

---

5. We have at least two kinds of evidence of what they knew. One is their own testimony: abundant scattered written evidence, in their own words, of their understanding of elitist elements in politics. The other is their unwillingness to defend pluralist orthodoxy from the challenge of elitist theory when that challenge was advanced, as it was during the 1960s and 1970s, against pluralist theory.

Another example of "arbitrary" constraints is PSI on policy proposals undertaken without reference to the ugliest aspects of the solutions—for example, their likely corruption through illegality. Foreign aid policy, for example, has been analyzed in academic circles with little attention to frequent charges from every corner of the underdeveloped world that much foreign assistance is siphoned off to the advantage of public officials and other favored groups. Medical care policy debate is only reluctantly—yet still not adequately coming to grips with illegal exploitation of medical care systems by physicians. And the study of crime in the U.S.A. has been distorted by the neglect of white-collar crime.

Is it possible that most pPSI, especially in the U.S.A., share a benign metaphysics that renders them unable to face some insalubrious aspects of society? Or are they caught in certain traditions passed down—indeed enforced —by the standardized instruction and examination procedures of graduate schools? Or do pPSI in fact respect certain rules of good form that prohibit discussion of certain topics, just as certain topics are proscribed around the dinner table in polite society? And if intellectual fashion accounts for some or all of the apparent arbitrariness of problem formulation, what makes fashion in the world of PSI?

One could declare the problem to be one of ideological bias in PSI. We choose, however, to cast a wider net—to try to be receptive to a wider variety of explanatory hypotheses, including but not limited to ideology.

Whatever the causes of the phenomenon—and the causes need to be researched—our hypothesis is that PSI is to a degree incapacitated in contributing to social problem solving because of its own metaphysics, fashions, traditions, and taboos. These incapacities need to be examined, not as amusing peripheral phenomena in PSI, but as important constraints on it.

These considerations make it seem that PSI follows culture and is imprisoned in it. To a great degree it is. But PSI is also a molder of culture. It seems quite likely that the social sciences and PSI have set their mark on the culture in distinct ways that influence problem setting and policy.[6]

6. See R. E. Lane, "The Decline of Politics and Ideology in a Knowledgeable Society," *American Sociological Review*, vol. 31 (October 1966).

8. Social Processes for Setting a Course for Professional Social Inquiry

It follows from all the issues raised in this book that wise choice and construction of research projects depend on many factors and pose no few or simple issues. It is not sufficient, for example, to defend choice of project simply by reference to a problem's social importance or to considerations of research feasibility. Taking into account, for example, such complications as that PSI is at best often only supplementary to other inputs into social problem solving or that it rarely achieves authoritative knowledge, wise choice requires an extremely complex analysis of relevant considerations. This being so, we suggest that project choice and design may require not a simple weighing of a few relevant issues but the development of complex guidelines for, and new understandings of, the use of PSI, as well as interactive processes for solving the very problem of what problems PSI should attack and in what ways.

Inferences about appropriate guidelines follow at every point from issues we have raised, some of which have been made explicit. One line of argument with which we must contend, however, suggests that satisfactory guidelines for project choice by pPSI are actually impossible or fruitless. On the one hand, so the argument goes, is the individualistic and often idiosyncratic nature of project choice by pPSI. Most projects, after all, are chosen by individuals operating under relatively few formal constraints. On the other hand are powerful informal social forces—taboos, ideologies, disciplinary values, and the like—which influence the choices of pPSI in ways they themselves hardly understand. If these are the circumstances under which PSI projects and methods are inevitably chosen, perhaps guidelines are implausible. How can pPSI's, or their institutions, or society itself, devise guidelines that would effectively redirect an enterprise which is at once loosely governed and at the same time deeply influenced by informal societal and cultural forces? Perhaps systematic guidelines are irrelevant, or a fantasy.

There are two other possibilities worth investigating. One is obvious: the possibility that by studying such issues as we have raised each pPSI can increase the sophistication of his PSI even if he cannot go far toward articulating guidelines. We would anticipate great gains along this line from such studies as we are proposing.

The other possibility is less obvious. It is that improvement in project choice might be achieved as a product of gains in the rationality of PSI as a "system" in which interaction plays a large role. The possibility may be raised as a question. Could PSI institutions and traditions be so changed as to promote greater wisdom in project choice without placing the entire burden on the uncoordinated efforts of isolated individuals? Are there ways of reorganizing the social system of PSI as opposed to reforming individual pPSI so that interaction would share with analysis some of the burden of solving the problem of what pPSI should study or research?

One answer to such a question is to invoke the intellectual guidance system sometimes thought to steer the natural sciences. The principal features of such a system are of two quite different kinds. One is that offsetting biases and parochialisms among individual scientists results in a distribution of research projects which, although not analyzed or chosen through analysis, is more defensible than the project choice of any single scientist. Hence an observer of the system would not look for evidence that each project was carefully chosen, only that the configuration of projects displayed some defensible pattern.

Countervailing irrationalities—your attending, for whatever reasons, to what I, for whatever reasons, have neglected—accomplish a collective rationality. The second feature is mutual criticism among scientists by which, despite the inability of any one scientist fully to justify his project choice, the level of thoughtfulness or sophistication with which projects are chosen can be greatly raised.

The most carefully thought out version of these possibilities is Michael Polanyi's. His thesis is that science is well guided by a mutually interactive process among scientists in which the "system" achieves a rationality superior to that of any individual in it.[1] His own model of the process is incomplete on many points and possibly incorrect on others. In principle, however, he may be right in arguing that under appropriate circumstances mutual adjustment can achieve defensible coordination and guidance of the complex processes of scientific choice. He points to the market as an example of a different but related kind of mutual adjustment in another area in which coordination is required. He suggests that a "hidden hand" may operate to guide science, even though it is a different hidden hand from Adam Smith's.

His idea of a "republic of science" does not, it should be noted, depend entirely on mutual criticism among scientists of projects and research results. But incentives to cogent criticism are part of the mechanism. Incentives are important because the notion of a self-regulating, mutually interactive system of guidance might be viable only insofar as there were strong incentives for criticism, as opposed to encouragement of cliqueishness, intellectual pork-barrelling, or other possible perversions. As for cogency, since criticism of any given scientific endeavor could occur along any number of dimensions, helpful criticism should

1. Michael Polanyi, "The Republic of Science: Its Political and Economic Theory," *Minerva* 1 (Autumn 1962): 54–73.

be salient and consistent. The success of such a system as Polanyi outlines might depend upon there being accepted criteria for criticism. It is widely believed that such criteria for criticizing project choice and results are given in the existing cumulative structure of scientific theory and research.

Sufficient incentives for cogent mutual criticism seem problematic in PSI. There are systematic interrelationships among pPSI (the journals, and reviews, informal interchange, conferences, the perpetuation of intellectual traditions through graduate training) which give guidance. Yet questions arise about the systematic effects of the interrelations, and especially about such "optimizing" tendencies as the Polanyi model specifies.

One problem with the Polanyi model is that he finds interaction among scientists alone to be the chief guidance and coordination system, leaving relatively little room, except as aberration, for interaction between scientists and other, such as practical problem solvers, engineers, government and foundation officials. The model thus appears to describe professional inquiry in little relation to the many other inputs into problem solving to which we have given great attention here. Because his approach does not take into account any interaction save that among scientists—framed as it was for the natural sciences and with the idea in mind of criticizing state guidance of scientific inquiry in Eastern Europe—his model raises various questions about whether other participants in interaction, for example, those with money and power, can be incorporated into such a system without corrupting it.

Our main point about Polanyi's model, though, is that good choice of project is not to be achieved wholly by understanding but rather by a combination of understanding or analysis and social interaction. Just as we have stressed that social problem solving requires understanding adapted to interactive problem solving—thus PSI combined with social interaction—so also we suggest, then, that solving the problem of which PSI projects should or should not be attempted calls finally for a combination of PSI and social interaction on that very issue. This is a good note on which to conclude. The burden of guiding PSI research projects cannot rest wholly on PSI understanding of the problem. We further acknowledge, therefore, that there are even limits to the profitability of studying such issues as we have outlined in these pages and to the efficacy of such new strategies for project choice and design as we have discussed.

Bibliography

The Bibliography begins with:

Reports of commissions and research groups

Bibliographies

Thereafter, citations to books and articles are classified. The categories do not appear in alphabetical order but are arranged in order of decreasing generality of subject matter. Thus citations grouped under the heading "Science and scientific method" come early in the Bibliography, while items under "Allocation of research funds and energies" come at the end.

The categories are:

Science and scientific method
Causal and interpretive explanation
History of science
Sociology of science; science and society
Social science and scientific method
Social science and research in social problem solving
Social science and research in public policy making
Essays and studies in specific disciplines:
    Anthropology
    Economics
    Political Science
    Psychology
    Sociology

Special topics:

Government support of social science and social research
Allocation of research funds and energies
Sociology of the scientific community

Entries in the Bibliography appear under only one heading. Assignment to a category is often arbitrary. We have often placed an entry in a higher rather than lower category to acknowledge the generality of its contribution to the literature.

Entries under Science and scientific method, History of science, and Sociology of science represent only a few of the items in those vast areas that are especially helpful in work on useful social science.

REPORTS OF COMMISSIONS AND RESEARCH GROUPS

National Academy of Sciences. *The Behavioral Sciences and the Federal Government*. Washington, D.C.: National Research Council, 1968.

National Academy of Sciences and the Social Research Council. *The Behavioral and Social Sciences: Outlook and Needs*. Englewood Cliffs, N.J.: Prentice-Hall, 1969.

National Academy of Sciences. *Basic Research and National Goals*. Washington, D.C.: Government Printing Office, March 1965.

National Science Board. *Knowledge and Action: Improving the Nation's Use of the Social Sciences*. Washington, D.C.: National Science Foundation, 1969.

U.S., Congress, House, Committee on Government Operations, *The Use of Social Research in Federal Domestic Programs*, 90th Cong., 1st sess. (Washington, D.C.: Government Printing Office, April 1967).

University of Michigan Institute for Social Research, Center for Research on Utilization of Scientific Knowledge.

National Academy of Sciences and National Research Council, Study Project on Social Research and Development.

BIBLIOGRAPHIES

American Association for the Advancement of Science. *Science for Society: A Bibliography*. 6th ed. Washington, D.C.: AAAS, 1976.

Brodbeck, May, ed. *Readings in the Philosophy of the Social Sciences*. New York: Macmillan, 1968, pp. 737–68.

Crawford, Elisabeth T. "The Sociology of the Social Sciences: An International Bibliography." *Social Science Information* 9 (1970) and biannually thereafter.

Crawford, Elisabeth T., and Biderman, Albert D., eds. *Social Scientists and International Affairs*. New York: John Wiley and Sons, 1969. Pages 285–324 contain an annotated bibliography on social science and public policy.

Fay, Brian. *Social Theory and Political Science* (London: Allen & Unwin, 1975), pp. 111–16.

Norton, Hugh S. *The Role of the Economist in Government* (Berkeley: McCutchan, 1969), pp. 239–41.

Orlans, Harold. *Contracting for Knowledge* (San Francisco: Jossey-Bass, 1973), pp. 263–77.

Seidel, Andrew D. *Strategic Decision-Making in Government: A Selected Bibliography*. Council of Planning Librarians, Exchange Bibliography #1326.

Storer, Norman W. *The Social System of Science*. New York: Holt, Rinehart and Winston, 1966. Pages 6–9 contain an annotated bibliography on the sociology of science; and pages 169–75 enlarge the bibliography without annotation.

BOOKS AND ARTICLES

Science and Scientific Method

Achinstein, Peter. *Law and Explanation*. New York: Oxford University Press, 1971.

Barnes, S. Barry, and Law, John. "Areas of Ignorance in Normal Science." *Sociological Review* 24 (February 1976).

Blalock, Jr., Hubert. *Causal Inferences in Nonexperimental Research*. Chapel Hill: University of North Carolina Press, 1964.

Blumer, Herbert. "Science Without Concepts." *The American Journal of Sociology* 36 (January 1931).

Bronowski, Jacob. *The Origins of Knowledge and Imagination*. New Haven: Yale University Press, 1978.

Campbell, Norman Robert. *What is Science?* New York: Dover, 1953.

Cohen, R. S.; Feyerabend, P. K.; and Wartofsky, M. W. eds. *Essays in Memory of Imre Lakatos*. Boston: Reidel, 1976.

Cournand, Andre, and Meyer, Michael. "The Scientist's Code." *Minerva* 14 (Spring 1976).

Gay, Hannah. "Radicals and Types: A Critical Comparison of the Methodologies of Popper and Lakatos and Their Use in the Resconstruction of Some 19th Century Chemistry." *Studies in History and Philosophy of Science* 7 (1967).

Harré, Rom, and Madden, E. H. "In Defence of Natural Agents." *The Philosophical Quarterly* 23 (April 1973).
————. "Natural Powers and Powerful Natures." *Philosophy* 48 (July 1973).
Harré, Rom. *The Principles of Scientific Thinking*. 2d ed. London: MacMillan, 1972.
Kisiel, Theodore, and Johnson, Galen. "New Philosophies of Science in the USA." *Zeitschrift für Allegemeine Wissenschaftstheorie* 5, no. 1 (1974).
Knight, Frank H. "Virtue and Knowledge: The View of Professor Polanyi." *Ethics* 59 (July 1949).
Kuhn, Thomas S. *The Structure of Scientific Revolutions*. 2d ed. Chicago: University of Chicago Press, 1970.
Lakatos, Imre, and Musgrave, Alan, eds. *Criticism and The Growth of Knowledge*. Cambridge: Cambridge University Press, 1970.
Magee, Brian. *Karl Popper*. New York: Viking Press, 1973.
Mulkay, M. J. "Three Models of Scientific Development." *Sociological Review* 23 (1975).
Nagel, Ernest. *Structure of Science*. New York: Harcourt, Brace and World, 1971.
Polanyi, Michael. *Personal Knowledge*. Chicago: University of Chicago Press, 1958.
Popper, Karl, and Eccles, John. *The Self and Its Brain*. New York: Springer Verlag, 1977.
Simon, Herbert A., "On the Definition of the Causal Relation." *Journal of Philosophy* 49 (July 1952). Reprinted in Simon, Herbert A. *Models of Man*. New York: John Wiley & Sons, 1957.
Toulmin, Stephen. "The Structure of Scientific Theories." In Frederick Suppe, ed., *The Search for Philosophic Understanding of Scientific Theories*. Urbana: University of Illinois Press, 1974.
Wolfle, Dael, ed. *Symposium on Basic Research*. Washington, D.C.: American Association for the Advancement of Science, 1959.
————. *Science and Public Policy*. Lincoln: University of Nebraska Press, 1959.
Zilsel, Edgar. "Physics and the Problem of Historico-Socio-

logical Laws." *Philosophy of Science* 8 (Autumn 1941). Reprinted in Feigl, Herbert, and Brodbeck, May. *Readings in the Philosophy of Science*. New York: Appleton-Century-Crofts, 1953.

Causal and Interpretive Explanation

Brandt, Richard, and Kim, Jaegwon. "Wants in Explanations of Actions." *Journal of Philosophy* 60 (July 1963).
Davidson, Donald. "Actions, Reasons and Causes." *Journal of Philosophy* 60 (November 1963). Reprinted in Brodbeck, May. *Readings in the Philosophy of the Social Sciences*. New York: MacMillan, 1968.
Goldman, Alvin I. *A Theory of Human Action*. Englewood Cliffs, N.J.: Prentice-Hall, 1970.
Skinner, Quentin. "Social Meaning and the Explanation of Social Action." In Laslett, Peter; Runciman, W. G.; and Skinner, Quentin. *Philosophy, Politics and Society*. New York: Barnes and Noble, 1972.

History of Science

Baritz, Loren. *The Servants of Power*. Middletown, Conn.: Wesleyan University Press, 1960.
Coser, Lewis. *Men of Ideas: A Sociologist's View*. New York: The Free Press, 1965.
Crombie, A. C., ed. *Scientific Change*. New York: Basic Books, 1963.
Crosland, M., ed. *The Emergence of Science in Western Europe*. New York: Science History Publications, 1976.
de Huszar, George B., ed. *The Intellectuals*. Glencoe, Ill.: The Free Press, 1960.
Gillespie, Charles. *The Edge of Objectivity: An Essay in the History of Scientific Ideas*. Princeton, N.J.: Princeton University Press, 1960.
Gilpin, Robert, and Wright, Christopher, eds. *Scientists and National Policy-Making*. New York: Columbia University Press, 1964.
Glazer, Nathan. "The Rise of Social Research in Europe." In Lerner, Daniel, ed. *The Human Meaning of the Social Sciences*. New York: Meridian Books, 1959.

Hall, A. R. "Merton Revisited." *History of Science* 2 (1963).
Holton, Gerald. "Scientific Research and Scholarship: Notes Toward the Design of Proper Scales." *Daedalus* 91 (Spring 1962).
Kaplan, Norman. "The Western European Scientific Establishment in Transition." *The American Behavioral Scientist* 6 (March/April 1962).
Lakatos, Imre. "History of Science and its Rational Reconstructions." *Boston Studies in the Philosophy of Science* 8 (1970).
Merton, Robert K. *Science, Technology and Society in Seventeenth Century England*. New York: Howard Fertig, 1970.
Orlans, Harold. "The Advocacy of Social Science in Europe and America." *Minerva* 14 (Spring 1976).
Shryock, Richard H. "American Indifference to Basic Science During the Nineteenth Century." In Shryock, Richard H. *Medicine in America: Historical Essays*. Baltimore: Johns Hopkins Press, 1966.
Toulmin, Stephen. "From Form to Function: Philosophy and History of Science in the 1950's and Now." *Daedalus* 1 (Summer 1977).

Sociology of Science; Science and Society

Barber, Bernard. *Science and the Social Order*. New York: The Free Press, 1952.
Barber, Bernard, and Hirsch, Walter, eds. *The Sociology of Science*. New York: The Free Press, 1967.
Ben-David, Joseph. "Scientific Growth: A Sociological View." *Minerva* 2 (Summer 1964).
———. *The Scientist's Role in Society*. Englewood Cliffs, N.J.: Prentice-Hall, 1971.
Churchman, C. West. *Challenge to Reason*. New York: Mc-Graw-Hill, 1968.
Daniels, George H. "The Pure-Science Ideal and Democratic Culture." *Science* 156 (June 30, 1967).
Dencik, Lars, ed. *Scientific Research and Politics*. Lund, Sweden: Student Literature, 1969.
Diesing, Paul. *Reason in Society*. Urbana: University of Illinois Press, 1962).
Dupre, J. Stefan, and Lakoff, Sanford. *Science and the Nation*.

Englewood Cliffs, N.J.: Prentice-Hall, 1962.

Frankel, Eugene. "Corpuscular Optics and the Wave Theory of Light: The Science and Politics of a Revolution in Physics." *Social Studies of Science* 6 (May 1976).

Kaplan, Norman. "The Sociology of Science." In Faris, Robert E., ed. *Handbook of Modern Sociology*. Chicago: Rand McNally, 1964.

Kaplan, Norman, ed. *Science and Society*. Chicago: Rand McNally, 1965.

Kecskemeti, Paul. *Sociological Aspects of the Information Process*. Santa Monica, Calif.: The RAND Corp., 1952.

Merton, Robert K. "The Sociology of Knowledge." In Gurvitch, Georges, and Moore, Wilbert E., eds. *Twentieth Century Sociology*. New York: The Philosophical Library, 1945.

Noble, David F. *America by Design: Science, Technology and the Rise of Corporate Capitalism*. New York: Alfred Knopf, 1977.

Primack, J. R., and von Hippel, Frank. *Advice and Dissent*. New York: Basic Books, 1974.

Roberts, Marc. "On the Nature and Condition of Social Science." *Daedalus* (Summer 1973).

Rose, Hilary, and Rose, Steven, eds. *The Political Economy of Science. Ideology of/in the Natural Sciences*. New York: Holmes and Meier, 1977.

Spiegel-Rösina, Ina-Susanne, and Price, Derek de Solla, eds. *Science, Technology and Society*. Beverly Hills, Calif.: Sage, 1977.

Veblen, Thorstein. "The Evolution of the Scientific Point of View." In Thorstein Veblen. *The Place of Science in Modern Civilization and other Essays*. New York: Viking Press, 1919.

Ziman, John. *Public Knowledge: The Social Dimension of Science*. Cambridge: Cambridge University Press, 1968.

Znaniecki, Florian. *The Social Role of the Man of Knowledge*. New York: Columbia University Press, 1940.

Social Science and Scientific Method

Bloor, David. *Knowledge and Social Imagery*. London: Routledge and Kegan Paul, 1976.

Boalt, Gunnar. *The Sociology of Research*. Carbondale: Southern Illinois University Press, 1969.

Brodbeck, May. *Readings in the Philosophy of the Social Sciences*. New York: MacMillan, 1968.

Freese, Lee. "Cumulative Sociological Knowledge." *American Sociological Review* 37 (August–December 1972).

Gouldner, Alvin. *Enter Plato: Classical Greece and the Origins of Social Theory*. New York: Basic Books, 1965.

Hart, H. L. A., and Honore, A. M. *Causation in the Law*. Oxford: Clarendon, 1959.

Helmer, Olaf, and Rescher, Nicholas. "The Epistemology of the Inexact Sciences." *Management Science* 6 (October 1959).

Homans, George C. *Social Behavior: Its Elementary Forms*. New York: Harcourt, Brace & World, 1961.

Kaplan, Abraham. *The Conduct of Inquiry*. San Francisco: Chandler, 1964.

Lerner, Daniel, ed. *The Human Meaning of the Social Sciences*. New York: Meridian Books, 1959.

Lundberg, George. *Can Science Save Us?* New York: Longmans, Green, 1947.

MacRae, Duncan. *The Social Function of Social Science*. New Haven: Yale University Press, 1976.

Machlup, Fritz. "Are the Social Sciences Really Inferior?" *Southern Economic Journal* 27 (January 1961).

Merton, Robert K. *Social Theory and Social Structure*, rev. ed. 1968. New York: The Free Press, 1957.

————. "Sociology of Social Problems." In Merton, Robert K., and Nisbet, Robert, eds. *Contemporary Social Problems*. 4th ed. New York: Harcourt, Brace & World, 1976.

Merton, Robert K., and Nisbet, Robert A., eds. *Contemporary Social Problems*. 2d ed. New York: Harcourt, Brace & World, 1966.

Mills, C. Wright. *The Sociological Imagination*. New York: Oxford University Press, 1959.

Moon, J. Donald. "The Logic of Political Inquiry: A Synthesis of Opposed Perspectives." In Greenstein, Fred I., and Polsby, Nelson W., eds. *Handbook of Political Science*, vol. 1. Reading, Mass.: Addison-Wesley, 1975.

Myrdal, Gunnar. *Value in Social Theory: A Selection of Essays on Methodology*. New York: Harper, 1958.

Schuetz, Alfred. "The Problem of Rationality in The Social World." *Economica* 10 (May 1943).

Simey, T. S. *Social Science and Social Purpose*. London: Constable, 1968.

Tribe, L. H.; Schelling, T. S.; and Voss, J., eds. *When Values Conflict*. Cambridge, Mass.: Ballinger, 1976.

Weber, Max. *The Methodology of the Social Sciences*. Translated and edited by Edward A. Shils, and Henry A. Finch. New York: Free Press of Glencoe, 1949.

Willer, David, and Willer, Judith. "Why Sociological Knowledge is Not Cumulative." *American Sociological Review* 37 (August–December 1972).

Wooton, Barbara. "The Long Term Impact of the Social Sciences on Democratic Political Practice." *Confluence* 3 (March 1954).

Zetterberg, Hans. L. *Social Theory and Social Practice*. New York: Bedminster Press, 1962.

Social Science and Research in Social Problem Solving

Almond, Gabriel, and Genco, Stephen J. "Clouds, Clocks, and the Study of Politics." *World Politics* 29 (July 1977).

Barton, Allen. "The Sociology of Reading Research." *Teachers College Record* 63 (November 1961).

Becker, Ernest. *Structure of Evil: An Essay on the Unification of the Science of Man*. New York: G. Braziller, 1968.

Bernstein, Richard. *The Restructuring of Social and Political Theory*. New York: Harcourt, Brace and Jovanovich, 1976.

Boulding, K. *The Impact of the Social Sciences*. New Brunswick, N.J.: Rutgers University Press, 1966.

Bressler, Marvin. "The Conventional Wisdom of Education and Sociology." In Page, Charles E., ed. *Sociology and Contemporary Education*. New York: Random House, 1963.

Campbell, Donald T. "Reforms as Experiments." *American Psychologist* 24 (April 1969).

Cherns, Albert. "Uses of the Social Science." *Human Relations* 27 (1968).

Coase, R. H. "The Market for Goods and the Market for Ideas." *The American Economic Review* 64 (May 1974).

Cohen, David K., and Garet, Michael S. "Reforming Educational Policy with Applied Social Research." *Harvard Educational Review* 45 (February 1975).

Crane, Diana. "Information Needs and Uses." *Annual Review of Information Science and Technology* 6 (1976).

Crawford, Elisabeth, and Perry, Norman, eds. *Demands for Social Knowledge*. London: Sage, 1976.

Crawford, Elisabeth, and Biderman, Albert D., eds. *Social Scientists and International Affairs*. New York: John Wiley & Sons, 1969.

Crick, Bernard. "What is Truth in Social Science?" *New Society* 3 (June 4, 1964).

Cullingworth, J. B. "The Politics of Research." In Cullingworth, J. B., ed. *Problems of Urban Society*, vol. 3. London: Allen and Unwin, 1973.

Deitchman, Seymour J. *The Best-Laid Schemes: A Tale of Social Research and Bureaucracy*. Ann Arbor: University of Michigan Press, 1977.

Deutsch, Karl W.; Platt, John; and Senghaas, Dieter. "Conditions Favoring Major Advances in Social Science." *Science* 171 (February 5, 1971).

Dewey, John. *The Quest for Certainty*. New York: Pulman, 1929.

————. "Liberating the Social Scientist: A Plea to Unshackle the Study of Man." *Commentary* 4 (October 1947).

Dickson, Paul. *Think Tanks*. New York: Atheneum, 1971.

Downey, Lawrence D., and Enns, Frederick, eds. *The Social Sciences and Educational Administration*. Edmonton, Alberta: Division of Educational Administration, University of Alberta, 1963.

Duke University School of Law. "The Courts, Social Science and School Desegregation," parts 1 and 2. *Law and Contemporary Problems* 39 (1975).

Etzioni, Amitai. *The Active Society*. New York: The Free Press, 1968.

Eulau, Heinz. "The Interventionist Synthesis." *American Journal of Political Science* 21 (May 1977).

Eversley, David. *The Planner in Society*. London: Faber, 1973.

Fay, Brian. *Social Theory and Political Practice*. London: Allen & Unwin, 1975.

Furner, Mary O. *Advocacy and Objectivity*. Lexington, Ky.: Published for the Organization of American Historians by the University Press of Kentucky, 1975.

Gerver, Israel, and Bensman, Joseph. "Towards a Sociology of Expertness." *Social Forces* 32 (March 1954).

Glock, Charles Y., et al. *Case Studies in Bringing Behavioral Science into Use*. Stanford, Calif.: Institute for Communication Research, Stanford University, 1961.

Goodwin, Leonard. *Can Social Science Help Solve National Problems? Welfare: A Case in Point*. New York: The Free Press, 1975.

Gouldner, Alvin W. "Explorations in Applied Social Science." *Social Problems* 3 (January 1956).

————. "Theoretical Requirements of the Applied Social Sciences." *American Sociological Review* 22 (February 1957).

Gross, Bertram M., ed. *Social Intelligence for America's Future*. Boston: Allyn and Bacon, 1969.

Habermas, J. *Toward a Rational Society*. London: Heinemann, 1971.

————. *Theory and Practice*. Boston: Beacon Press, 1973.

Hägerstrand, Torsten. *Innovation Diffusion as a Spatial Process*. Chicago: University of Chicago Press, 1967.

Harter, Carl L. "The Power Roles of Intellectuals: An Introductory Statement." *Sociology and Social Research* 48 (January 1964).

Hauser, Philip M. "Are the Social Sciences Ready?" *American Sociological Review* 2 (August 1946).

Havelock, Ronald G., in collaboration with Guskin, Alan; Frohman, Mark; Havelock, Mary; Hill, Marjorie; and Huber, Janet. *Planning for Innovation: Through Dissemination and Utilization of Knowledge*. Ann Arbor: University of Michigan Press, 1977.

Herring, Pendleton, et al. *Research for Public Policy*. Washington, D.C.: Brookings Institution, 1966.

Hirschman, Albert O. "The Search for Paradigms as a Hindrance to Understanding." *World Politics* 22 (April 1970).

Hirschman, Albert O., and Lindblom, Charles E. "Economic Development, Research and Development, Policy Making: Some Converging Views." *Behavioral Science* 7 (April 1962).

Hodgson, Godfrey. "Do Schools Make a Difference?" *Atlantic* 231 (March 1973).

Horowitz, Irving L. *The Use and Abuse of Social Science*. Rev. ed. New Brunswick, N.J.: Transaction Books, 1975.

Horowitz, Irving L., ed. *The Rise and Fall of Project Camelot*. Cambridge: MIT Press, 1967.

Janowitz, M. *Political Conflict*. Chicago: University of Chicago Press, 1970.

Kelly, George A. "The Expert as Historical Actor." *Daedalus* 92 (Summer 1963).

Kelman, Herbert C. "The Social Consequences of Social Research: A New Social Issue." *The Journal of Social Issues* 21 (July 1965).

Leighton, Alexander H. *Human Relations in a Changing World: Observations on the Use of the Social Sciences*. New York: E. P. Dutton and Co., 1949.

Lane, Robert E. "The Decline of Politics and Ideology in a Knowledgeable Society." *American Sociological Review* 31 (October 1966).

Likert, Rensis, and Lippitt, Ronald. "The Utilization of Social Science." In Festinger, Leon, and Katz, Daniel, eds., *Research Methods in the Behavioral Sciences*. New York: The Dryden Press, 1953.

Lobkowicz, Nikolaus. *Theory and Practice: History of a Concept from Aristotle to Marx*. Notre Dame, Ind.: University of Notre Dame Press, 1967.

Lindblom, Charles E. *Politics and Markets*. New York: Basic Books, 1977.

Lindblom, Charles E., and Braybrooke, David. *A Strategy of Decision*. New York: The Free Press, 1970.

Lindblom, Charles E. *The Intelligence of Democracy*. New York: The Free Press, 1965.

London, Ivan D. "Convergent and Divergent Amplification and Its Meaning for Social Science. *Psychological Reports* 41 (1977).

Lynd, Robert S. *Knowledge for What?* Princeton, N.J.: Princeton University Press, 1948.

Majone, Giandomenico. "The Feasibility of Social Policies." *Policy Sciences* 6 (1975).

————. "The ABC's of Constraint Analysis." *Russell Sage Foundation Working Paper* No. 2 (1977).

Mannheim, K. *Ideology and Utopia*. New York: Harcourt, Brace & World, 1936.

Mills, C. Wright. *The Sociological Imagination*. New York: Oxford University Press, 1959.

Moore, Barrington. "Strategy in Social Science. In Moore, Barrington. *Political Power and Social Theory*. New York: Harper & Row, 1965.

Moynihan, Daniel P. *Maximum Feasible Misunderstanding*. New York: The Free Press, 1969.

National Research Council Advisory Commission for Assessment of University Based Institutes for Research on Poverty. "Policy and Program Research in a University Setting." Washington, D.C.: National Academy of Sciences, 1971.

Nelkin, Dorothy. *Technical Decisions and Democracy: European Experiments in Public Participation*. Beverly Hills, Calif.: Sage, 1977.

Nelson, Richard R. *The Moon and the Ghetto*. New York: W. W. Norton & Co., 1977.

Orlans, Harold. *Contracting for Knowledge*. San Francisco: Jossey-Bass, 1973.

Perlmutter, Howard B. *Towards a Theory and Practice of Social Architecture*. London: Tavistock, 1965.

Podell, Lawrence. "Social Research and Public Welfare." *Mandate for Research*. Washington, D.C.: American Public Welfare Association, 1965.

Polanyi, Michael. "The Republic of Science: Its Political and Economic Theory." *Minerva* 1 (Autumn 1962).

————. *Science, Faith, and Society*. London: Oxford University Press, 1946.

Popper, Karl R. *The Open Society and Its Enemies*. 5th ed., rev. Princeton, N.J.: Princeton University Press, 1966.

Price, Don K. *Government and Science*. New York: New York University Press, 1954.

————. *The Scientific Estate*. Cambridge, Mass.: Harvard University, Press, 1965.

Raab, E., and Selznick, G. J. *Major Social Problems*. 2d ed New York: Harper & Row, 1964.

Radom, Michael. *The Social Scientist in American Industry.* New Brunswick, N.J.: Rutgers University Press, 1970.

Rainwater, Lee, and Yancey, William L., *The Moyhnihan Report and the Politics of Controversy.* Cambridge, Mass.: MIT Press, 1967.

RAND Corporation. *How Effective Is Schooling?* Englewood Cliffs, N.J.: Educational Technology Publications, 1974.

Reiss, Albert J., Jr. "Putting Sociology into Policy." *Social Problems* 17 (Winter 1970).

Rescher, Nicholas. "The Role of Values in Social Science Research." In Frankel, Charles, ed. *Controversies and Decisions.* New York: Russell Sage, 1976.

Rivlin, Alice. *Systematic Thinking and Social Action.* Washington, D.C.: Brookings Institution, 1971.

―――. "How Can Experiments be More Useful?" *American Economic Review* 64 (May 1974).

Rogin, Michael. *The Intellectuals and McCarthy.* Cambridge, Mass.: MIT Press, 1967.

Rothman, Jack. *Planning and Organizing for Social Change.* New York: Columbia University Press, 1974.

Rowe, A. P. "From Scientific Idea to Practical Use." *Minerva* 2 (Spring 1964).

Scheingold, Stuart. *The Politics of Rights.* New Haven: Yale University Press, 1977.

Schwartz, Benjamin I. "The Rousseau Strain in the Contemporary World." *Daedalus* (Summer 1978).

Sherwin, C. W., and Isenson, R. S. "Project Hindsight." *Science* 156 (June 1967).

Shils, Edward. *The Torment of Secrecy.* New York: The Free Press, 1956.

Sjoberg, Gideon, ed. *Ethics, Politics and Social Research.* Cambridge, Mass.: Schenkman Publishing, 1967.

Smith, Bruce L. R. *The RAND Corporation.* Cambridge, Mass.: Harvard University Press, 1966.

Storm, Norman. "Basic vs. Applied Research." *Indian Sociological Bulletin* 2 (October 1964).

Trist, Eric. "Types of Output Mix of Research Organizations and Their Complementarity." In Cherns, A. B.; Sinclair, R.; and Jenkins, W. I., eds, *Social Science and Government:*

Policies and Problems. London: Tavistock, 1972.

U.K., *Report of the Committee on the Management and Control of Research and Development* (HMSO, 1961).

U.S., Congress, Senate, Committee on Government Operations, *Specialists and Generalists: A Selection of Readings*, 90th Cong., 2d sess. (Washington, D.C.: Government Printing Office, 1968).

Vickers, Geoffrey, *Value Systems and Social Process*. New York: Basic Books, 1968.

Weber, Max. "Politics as a Vocation" (1918). Reprinted in Gerth, H.H., and Mills, C. Wright. *From Max Weber: Essays in Sociology*. New York: Oxford University Press, 1946.

Wesson, Robert G. *Why Marxism?* New York: Basic Books, 1975.

Wilensky, Harold L. *Organizational Intelligence*. New York: Basic Books, 1967.

Wirth, Louis. "Responsibility of Social Sciences." *Annals of the American Academy of Political and Social Science* 249 (January 1948).

Wooton, Barbara. *Social Science and Pathology*. London: Allen and Unwin, 1959.

Zircher, Louis A., and Bonjean, Charles A. eds. *Planned Social Intervention*. New York: Chandler, 1970.

Social Science and Research in Public Policy Making

Abt, Clark, ed. *The Evaluation of Social Programs*. Beverly Hills, Calif.: Sage, 1977.

Anderson, James. *Cases in Public Policy Making*. New York: Praeger, 1976.

Archibald, K. A. "Three Views of the Expert's Role in Policy-Making." *Policy Science* 1 (Spring 1970).

Banner, David; Doctors, Samuel; and Gordon, Andrew. *The Politics of Social Program Evaluation*. Cambridge: Ballinger Press, 1975.

Barnett, M. J. *The Politics of Legislation*. London: Weidenfeld & Nicolson, 1969.

Bauer, Raymond A., and Gergen, Kenneth, J., eds. *The Study of Policy Formation*. New York: The Free Press, 1968.

Brewer, Garry D., and Kakalik, James S. *Handicapped Children: Strategies for Improving Services*. New York: Mc-Graw-Hill, 1978.

Brewer, Garry D., and Blair, Bruce G. "War Games and National Security: With a Grain of SALT." *Bulletin of Atomic Scientists*, forthcoming.

Brewer, Garry D. "Analysis of Complex Systems: An Experiment and Its Implications for Policymaking." In LaPorte, Todd R., ed. *Organized Social Complexity: Challenge to Politics and Policy*. Princeton: Princeton University Press, 1975.

Caplan, Nathan; Morrison, Andrea; and Stambaugh, Russell J. *The Use of Social Science Knowledge in Policy Decisions at the National Level*. Center for Research on Utilization of Scientific Knowledge, Institute for Social Research, University of Michigan, Ann Arbor, Michigan, 1975.

Cohen, David K., and Garet, Michael S. "Reforming Educational Policy with Applied Social Research." *Harvard Educational Review* 45 (February 1975).

Coleman, James S. "Policy Research in the Social Sciences." Morristown, N.J.: General Learning Press, 1972.

Cronin, Thomas E., and Thomas, Norman C. "Educational Policy Advisors and the Great Society." Washington, D.C.: Brookings Institution, 1970.

Cronin, Thomas E., and Greenberg, Sanford D., eds. *The Presidential Advisory System*. New York: Harper & Row, 1969.

Donnison, D. "Research for Policy." *Minerva* 10 (October 1972).

Dye, Thomas. *Understanding Public Policy*. 2d ed. Englewood Cliffs, N.J.: Prentice-Hall, 1975.

Dror, Yehezkel. *Design for Policy Sciences*. New York: American Elsevier, 1971.

———. *Public Policy Making Reexamined*. San Francisco: Chandler, 1968.

———. *Ventures in Policy Sciences*. New York: American Elsevier, 1971.

Edwards, George C. III, and Sharkansky, Ira. *The Policy Predicament*. San Francisco: W. H. Freeman, 1978.

Eidell, Terry L., and Kitchel, Joanne N., eds. *Knowledge Production and Utilization in Educational Administration*.

Eugene, Ore.: University of Oregon Center for the Advanced Study of Educational Administration, 1968.

Frankel, Charles, ed. *Controversies and Decisions: The Social Sciences and Public Policy*. New York: Russell Sage, 1976.

Freeman, Howard E., ed. *Social Research and Social Policy*. Englewood Cliffs, N.J.: Prentice-Hall, 1969.

Goldenweiser, E.A. *Translating Facts into Policy*. New York: National Bureau of Economic Research, 1946.

Greenberger, Martin; Crenson, Matthew; and Crissey, Brian L. *Models in Policy Process*. New York: Russell Sage, 1976.

Gregg, Phillip M., ed. *Problems in Theory in Policy Analysis*. Lexington, Mass.: D.C. Heath & Co., 1976.

Haverman, Robert H., and Margolis, Julius. *Public Expenditures and Policy Analysis*. Chicago: Markham, 1970.

Heclo, Hugh. "Review Article: Policy Analysis." *British Journal of Political Science* 2 (January 1972).

Horowitz, Irving L. *The Use and Abuse of Social Science*. 2d ed. New Brunswick, N.J.: Transaction Books, 1975.

————. "Social Science Mandarins: Policymaking as a Political Formula." *Policy Sciences* 1 (Fall 1970).

Janowitz, Morris. "Sociological Models and Social Policy." *Archiv für Rechtsund Sozialphilosophie* 55 (August 1969).

Jones, Charles O. "Why Congress Can't Do Policy Analysis (or words to that effect)." *Policy Analysis* 2 (1976).

Kecskemeti, Paul. "The 'Policy Sciences': Aspiration and Outlook." *World Politics* 4 (July 1952).

————. *Utilization of Social Science Research in Shaping Policy Decisions*. Santa Monica, Calif.: The RAND Corporation, April 24, 1961.

Kelly, George. "The Expert as Historical Actor." *Daedalus* 92 (Summer 1963).

Komarovsky, M., ed. *Sociology and Public Policy: The Case of Presidential Commissions*. New York: Elsevier, 1975.

Landau, Martin. "The Proper Domain of Policy Analysis." *American Journal of Political Science* 2 (May 1977).

Lasswell, Harold. *A Preview of the Policy Sciences*. New York: American Elsevier, 1971.

Lerner, Allan W. "Experts, Politicians, and Decisionmaking in the Technological Society." Morristown, N.J.: General Learning Press, 1976.

Lerner, Daniel, and Lasswell, Harold D., eds. *The Policy Sciences: Recent Developments in Scope and Method.* Stanford, Calif.: Stanford University Press, 1951.

Levin, Henry M. "Education, Chances, and the Courts: The Role of Social Science Evidence." *Law and Contemporary Problems* 39 (Spring 1975).

Lynn, Laurence J., ed. *Knowledge and Policy: The Uncertain Connection.* Washington, D.C.: National Academy of Sciences, 1978.

Lindblom, Charles E. "The Science of 'Muddling Through,' " *Public Administration Review* 19 (Spring 1959).

———. *The Policy-Making Process.* Englewood Cliffs, N.J.: Prentice-Hall, 1968.

Lompe, Klaus. "The Role of the Social Scientist in the Processes of Policy-Making." *Social Science Information* 7 (December 1968).

Majone, Giandomenico. "Policies on Theories." Paper presented at the Joint National TIMS/ORSA Meeting, San Francisco, May 9–11, 1977. Unpublished.

———. "The Uses of Policy Analysis." In *The Future and the Past: Essays on Programs.* New York: Russell Sage Foundation, 1977.

Meltsner, Arnold J. *Policy Analysts in the Bureaucracy.* Berkeley: University of California Press, 1976.

Merton, Robert K. "The Role of Applied Social Science in the Formation of Policy." *Philosophy of Science* 16 (July 1949).

Nagel, S. S., ed. *Policy Studies and the Social Sciences.* Lexington, Mass.: Lexington Books, 1975.

Olson, Mancur. "An Analytic Framework for Social Reporting and Policy Analysis." *The Annals of the American Academy of Political and Social Science* 388 (March 1970).

Rein, M. *Social Science and Social Policy.* New York: Penguin, 1976.

Ridley, F. F. "Policy-Making Science." *Political Studies* 18 (June 1970).

Rivlin, Alice M. *Systematic Thinking for Social Action.* Washington, D.C.: Brookings Institution, 1971.

Rondinelli, Dennis A. "Public Planning and Political Strategy." *Long Range Planning* 9 (April 1976).

Rossi, Peter, and Williams, Walter, eds. *Evaluating Social Pro-*

gram. Seminar Press, 1972.

Sapolsky, Harvey M. *The Polaris System Development*. Cambridge, Mass.: Harvard University Press, 1972.

Schick, Allen. "The Supply and Demand for Analysis on Capitol Hill." *Policy Analysis* 2 (January 1976).

Schultze, Charles L. *The Politics and Economics of Public Spending*. Washington, D.C.: Brookings Institution, 1968.

Self, Peter J. O. *Econocrats and the Policy Process*. London: MacMillan, 1976.

Sharkansky, Ira, ed. *Policy Analysis in Political Science*. Chicago: Markham, 1970.

Smith, Bruce L. R. "Strategic Expertise and National Security Policy." In Montgomery, John D., and Smithies, Arthur, eds. *Public Policy*. Cambridge, Mass.: Harvard University Press, 1964.

Stokey, Edith, and Zeckhauser, Richard. *A Primer for Policy Analysis*. New York: W. W. Norton & Co., 1978.

U.K. Department of Education and Science, *Report of the Committee on Social Studies* (Command 2660 HMSO, 1965).

U.S., Congress, Senate, Commission on the Operation of the Senate, *Policy Analysis on Major Issues*, 94th Cong., 2d sess. (Washington, D.C.: Government Printing Office, 1977).

U.S., Comptroller General, Report to the Congress, *Social Research and Development of Limited Use to National Policymakers* (Washington, D.C.: U.S. General Accounting Office, April 4, 1977).

U.S., Congress, House, Committee on Government Operations, *The Use of Social Research in Federal Domestic Programs* 4 (April 1967).

U.S., Congress, House, Committee on Government Operations, *The Use of Social Research in Federal Domestic Programs*, 90th Cong., 1st sess. (Washington, D.C.: Government Printing Office, 1967).

Weiss, Carol H. *Evaluation Research*. Englewood Cliffs, N.J.: Prentice-Hall, 1972.

———. *Using Social Research in Public Policy Making*. Lexington, Mass.: D.C. Heath & Co., 1977.

Weiss, Carol H., ed. Symposium on "The Research Utilization Quandary." *Policy Studies Journal* (Spring 1976).

Wildavsky, Aaron. *Speaking Truth to Power: The Art and Craft of Policy Analysis.* Boston: Little, Brown, Winter 1979.
———. *Budgeting: A Comparative Theory of Budgetary Processes.* Boston: Little, Brown, 1975.
Wildavsky, Aaron; Levy, Frank; and Meltsner, Arnold. *Urban Outcomes.* Berkeley: University of California Press, 1974.
Wildavsky, Aaron, and Caiden, Naomi. *Planning and Budgeting in Poor Countries.* New York: John Wiley & Sons, 1973.
Wilkins, Leslie T. *Social Policy, Action, and Research.* London: Associated Book Publishers, 1967.
Williams, Walter. *Social Policy Research and Analysis.* New York: American Elsevier, 1971.

Essays and Studies in Specific Disciplines

ANTHROPOLOGY

Diamond, Stanley. "Anthropology in Question." In Hymes, Dell. *Reinventing Anthropology.* New York: Random House, 1969.
Hymes, Dell. "The Use of Anthropology: Critical, Political, Personal." In Hymes, Dell. *Reinventing Anthropology.* New York: Random House, 1969.

ECONOMICS

Blaug, Mark. "Kuhn *vs.* Lakatos *or* Paradigms versus Research Programmes in The History of Economics." In Latsis, Spiro J., ed. *Method and Appraisal in Economics.* Cambridge: Cambridge University Press, 1976.
Dunlop, John T. "Policy Decisions and Research in Economics and Industrial Relations." *Industrial and Labor Relations Review* 30 (April 1977).
Flash, Edward S., Jr. *Economic Advice and Presidential Leadership: The Council of Economic Advisors.* New York: Columbia University Press, 1965.
Hutchison, T. W. *Knowledge and Ignorance in Economics.* Chicago: University of Chicago Press, 1977.
Johnson, Harry G. "National Styles in Economic Research: The United States, The United Kingdom, Canada, and Various European Countries." *Daedalus* 102 (Spring 1973).

————. "Individual and Social Choice." In Robinson, William, ed. *Man and the Social Sciences*. Beverly Hills, Calif.: Sage, 1972.

————. "The Keynesian Revolution and the Monetarist Counter-Revolution." *The American Economic Review* 61 (May 1971); also, *Encounter* 36 (April 1971).

Johr, W. A., and Singer, H. W. *The Role of the Economist as Official Adviser*. London: Allen & Unwin, 1955.

Letwin, William. *The Origins of Scientific Economics*. Garden City, N.J.: Doubleday, 1965.

Norton, Hugh S. *Role of the Economist in Government Policy Making*. Berkeley, Calif.: McCutchan, 1968.

Perlman, Mark. "Reflections on Methodology, Persuasion and Machlup." In Dreyer, Jacob S., ed. *Breadth and Depth in Economics: Fritz Machlup, the Man and His Ideas*. Lexington, Mass.: Lexington Books, 1978.

Salant, Walter S. *Some Intellectual Contributions of the Truman Council of Economic Advisors to Policy-Making*. Washington, D.C.: Brookings Institution, 1973.

Tobin, James. *National Economic Policy*. New Haven: Yale University Press, 1966.

POLITICAL SCIENCE

Austin, Ranney, ed. *Political Science and Public Policy*. Chicago: Markham Publishing Co., 1968.

Dye, Thomas. "Policy Analysis and Political Science." *Policy Studies Journal* 1 (Winter 1972).

Eckstein, Harry. "Political Science and Public Policy." In Pool, Ithiel de Sola, ed. *Contemporary Political Science: Toward Empirical Theory*. New York: McGraw-Hill, 1967.

Kirkpatrick, Evron M. "Toward a More Responsible Two-Party System: Political Science, Policy Science, or Pseudo-Science?" *American Political Science Review* (December 1971).

Melanson, Philip H. "The Political Science Profession." *Politics and Society* 2 (Summer 1972).

Melanson, Philip. *Political Science and Political Knowledge*. Washington, D.C.: Public Affairs Press, 1975.

PSYCHOLOGY

Caplan, Nathan, and Nelson, Stephen D. "On Being Useful: The Nature and Consequences of Psychological Research on Social Problems." *American Psychologist* 199 (March 1973).
Cronback, Lee J. "Five Decades of Public Controversy Over Mental Testing." *American Psychologist* 30 (January 1975).
Korten, Frances F. et al., eds. *Psychology and the Problems of Society.* Washington, D.C.: American Psychological Association, 1970.
Mackie, R. R., and Christensen, P. R. *Translation and Application of Psychological Research.* Technical Report 716–1. Santa Barbara Research Park, Goleta, California Human Factors Research, Inc., 1967.

SOCIOLOGY

Birnbaum, Norman. *Toward a Critical Sociology.* New York: Oxford University Press, 1971.
Blackburn, Robin, ed. *Ideology in Social Science, Readings in Critical Social Theory.* 1st American ed. New York: Pantheon Books, 1972.
Bottomore, T. B. *Sociology.* London: Allen and Unwin, 1962.
Bramsom, Leon. *The Political Context of Sociology.* Princeton, N.J.: Princeton University Press, 1961.
Gans, Herbert J. "Urban Poverty and Social Planning." In Lazarsfeld, P.; Sewell, W.; and Wilensky, H., eds. *The Uses of Sociology.* New York: Basic Books, 1967.
Gouldner, Alvin W. *The Coming Crisis of Western Sociology.* New York: Basic Books, 1970.
Gouldner, Alvin W., and Miller, S. M. *Applied Sociology: Opportunities and Problems.* New York: The Free Press, 1965.
Halmos, Paul, ed. *The Sociology of Sociology.* Keele, Eng.: University of Keele, 1970.
Lazarsfeld, P. *An Introduction to Applied Sociology.* New York: American Elsevier, 1975.
Lazarsfeld, P.; Sewell, W.; and Wilensky, H., eds. *The Uses of Sociology.* New York: Basic Books, 1967.
Ogburn, William F. "Some Observations on Sociological Re-

search." In Duncan, Otis Dudley, ed. *William F. Ogburn on Culture and Social Change*. Chicago: University of Chicago Press, 1964.

Pettigrew, Thomas F. "Sociological Consulting in Race Relations." *American Sociologist* 6, Supplementary Issue (June 1971).

Shils, Edward A. "The Calling of Sociology." In Parsons, Talcott, et al., eds. *Theories of Society: Foundation of Modern Sociological Theory*, vol. 2. New York: Free Press of Glencoe, 1961.

Shoslak, Arthur B., ed. *Sociology in Action*. Homewood, Ill.: Dorsey Press, 1966.

SPECIAL TOPICS

Government Support of Social Science and Social Research

Alpert, Harry. "Congressmen, Social Scientists, and Attitudes Toward Federal Support of Social Science Research." *American Sociological Review* 23 (December 1958).

Biderman, Albert, and Sharp, Laure. *The Competitive Evaluation Research Industry*. Washington, D.C.: Bureau of Social Science Research, 1972.

Beals, Ralph L. *Politics of Social Research*. Chicago: Alding, 1969.

Boffey, Phillip M. *The Brain Bank of America*. New York: McGraw-Hill, 1975.

Cherns, Albert; Sinclair, R.; and Jenkins, W. I., eds. *Social Science and Government*. London: Tavistock, 1972.

Dupree, A. Hunter. *Science in the Federal Government*. Cambridge, Mass.: Harvard University Press, 1957.

Horowitz, Irving L., and Katz, James E. *Social Science and Public Policy in the U.S.* New York: Praeger, 1975.

Lakoff, Sanford A., ed. *Knowledge and Power*. New York: The Free Press, 1966.

Lyons, Gene M., ed. *Social Science and the Federal Government*. The Annals of the American Academy of Political and Social Science 394, March 1971.

———. *Social Research and Public Policies: The Dartmouth/ OECD Conference*. Hanover, N.H.: Public Affairs Center, Dartmouth College, 1975.

Lyons, Gene M. *The Uneasy Partnership: Social Science and the Federal Government in the Twentieth Century.* New York: Russell Sage, 1965.

OECD. *The Social Sciences and the Policies of Governments.* Paris: OECD, 1966.

Parsons, Talcott. "The Science Legislation and the Role of the Social Sciences." *American Sociological Review* 11 (December 1946).

Price, Don K. *Government and Science: Their Dynamic Relation in American Democracy.* New York: New York University Press, 1954.

Sapolsky, Harvey. "Science Policy." In Greenstein, Fred I., and Polsby, Nelson W., eds. *The Handbook of Political Science*, vol. 8. Reading, Mass.: Addison-Wesley, 1975.

Tavistock Institute. *Social Research and a National Policy for Science.* London: Tavistock Institute, 1964.

U.S. National Resources Committee, Science Committee, *Research—A National Resource* (Washington, D.C.: U.S. Government Printing Office, 1938).

Useem, Michael. "Government Influence on the Social Science Paradigm." *The Sociological Quarterly* 17 (Spring 1976).

Allocation of Research Funds and Energies

Baker, William O. "The Paradox of Choice." In Wolfle, Dael, ed. *Symposium on Basic Research.* Washington, D.C.: American Association for the Advancement of Science, 1959.

Boulding, Kenneth E. "The Misallocation of Intellectual Resources in Economics." In Horowitz, Irving Louis, ed. *The Use and Abuse of Social Science.* New Brunswick, N.J.: Transaction Books, 1975.

Carter, C. F. "The Distribution of Scientific Effort." *Minerva* 1 (Winter 1963).

Handler, P., "Scientific Choice and Scientific Priorities in Biomedical Research." Paper presented at the Second NIH International Symposium, Williamsburg, V., March 1, 1965.

Maddox, John. "Choice and the Scientific Community." *Minerva* 2 (Winter 1964).

Nelson, Richard R. "The Simple Economics of Basic Scientific Research." *Journal of Political Economy* 67 (June 1959).

Oppenheimer, Robert J. "The Importance of New Knowledge." In Wolfle, Dael, ed. *Symposium on Basic Research*. Washington, D.C.: American Association for the Advancement of Science, 1959.

Rowe, A. P. "From Scientific Idea to Practical Use." *Minerva* 2 (Spring 1964).

Toulmin, Stephen. "The Complexity of Scientific Choice: A Stocktaking." *Minerva* 2 (Spring 1964).

Weinberg, Alvin M. "Criteria for Scientific Choice." *Minerva* 1 (Winter 1963).

———. *Reflections on Big Science*. Cambridge: MIT Press, 1967.

Sociology of the Scientific Community

Crane, Diana. "Scientists at Major and Minor Universities: A Study of Productivity and Recognition." *American Sociological Review* 30 (October 1965).

———. "Social Structure in a Group of Scientists: A Test of The 'Invisible College' Hypothesis." *American Sociological Review* 34 (June 1969).

Cooley, William. *Career Development of Scientists: An Overlapping Longitudinal Study*. Cambridge, Mass.: Graduate School of Education, Harvard University, 1963.

Hagstrom, Warren O. *The Scientific Community*. New York: Basic Books, 1965.

Kubie, Lawrence. "Some Unsolved Problems of the Scientific Career." *American Scientist* 61 (October 1953).

Mullins, N.C. "Social Networks among Biological Scientists." Ph.D. dissertation, Harvard University, 1966.

———. "The Micro-Structure of an Invisible College: The Phage Group." Paper delivered at annual meeting of American Sociological Association, Boston, Mass., 1968).

Price, D. J., and Beaver, D. de B. "Collaboration in an Invisible College." *American Psychologist* 21 (November 1966).

Storer, Norman W. *The Social System of Science*. New York: Holt, Rinehart and Winston, 1966.

Wilson, Logan. *The Academic Man*. New York: Oxford University Press, 1942.

Index

Academic social science, 7, 8, 78–79
Analytical problem solving, 8–9, 10, 11, 19; for business problems, 59; definition of, 20, 24; interaction as alternative to, 20–21; models of, 29; PSI bias toward, 30–39; relation to interactive problem solving, 20–21, 26–29; in social sciences, 10–11
Argument, contrasted with proof, 81
Arrow, Kenneth, 15
Art, PSI as, 84
Attitude change, through social learning, 18–19
Authoritativeness, 40; alternatives to, 73–85; applied to normative issues, 45–47; and conclusiveness, 41–42; and defining problems, 49–50; and divergence of research results, 47–49; failures of, 45–53; independent and dependent, 42–43, 49, 52–53; misperceptions about, 43–44; and nonrational responses to PSI, 45; and obsolescence of knowledge, 50–52; ordinary knowledge as basis for, 43; problems of, 36–39; and PSI incompetence in normative issues, 45–46; types of 42–43, 49, 52–53

Bargaining, 33
Bottlenecks, 67
Brahe, Tycho, 16
Business, interactive problem solving in, 22–23, 59
By-product problem solving, 56–58

Campbell, Donald T., 17
Casual empiricism, ordinary knowledge and, 12

Casual perception, contrasted with scientific observation, 15–16
City planning, and interactive problem solving, 61–62
Client relationship, 2, 69
Coin tossing, 21, 24, 27
Coleman, James, 15, 89
Common sense, as basis of ordinary knowledge, 12
Conclusiveness of results, 40, 41–42
Constraints on PSI, 93–95, 97
Cost-effectiveness analysis, 90
Craft, 13n
Crime, 20, 21, 25, 64
Crisis, 67
Cumulation of knowledge, 50–52, 86

Darwin, Charles, 16
Data gatherings, 83–84
Definition of problems, 49–50, 56; constraints on, 93–95
Delegation, 23, 25
Democracy and PSI, 69–71
De Tocqueville, Alexis, 16
Dewey, John, 4, 73
Divergence, 47–49
Dror, Yehezkel, 38–39
Dunlop, John, 47

Economic theory: adaptation to interaction, 61; lag in application of, 79–80; obsolescence of, 51
Elections, 21. *See also* Voting
Empiricism, in normative analysis, 11, 46, 47n
Energy conservation, 18, 55, 56
Engineering, social, 74–76
Enlightenment, as alternative role for PSI, 73–81

127